Ceramic Sculpture

Cat Group (25″ high). Terra cotta, solid arch construction. Glazed and fired in oxidation to cone 10.

CERAMIC SCULPTURE

Betty Davenport Ford

Reinhold Publishing Corporation
New York
an Art Horizons book

For my parents, Alfred L. Davenport and Nettie Blocker Davenport, and my husband Harold H. Ford, whose interest and encouragement has motivated and sustained my efforts.

738.1
F75c

47799
August, 1964

Contents

CERAMIC SCULPTURE—WHAT IT IS

Shaped by the hands, sensitive to the slightest pressure of the fingers, fired at incandescent heat to endure for centuries —this is ceramic sculpture. A delightful, flexible medium, its possibilities range from the solid, monolithic shape hollowed out from the back or bottom, through the multiple-form composition with voids between the forms, to the free-form sculpture which concentrates on a single shape spontaneously elaborated, such as coils of clay laid up in arches like a bridge. For the beginner and student the variety of exciting small forms—human, animal, plant, and abstract—that can be created from clay is unlimited. For the advanced student there are larger and more complex projects, such as fountains and other architectural sculptures, either composed of many smaller units fired separately and stacked one upon another, or built in one piece; the extent of these projects is limited only by the capacity of the kiln available. An incredible range of colors and finishes which give richness and excitement to the work of art are available to the ceramic sculptor.

The relative speed of execution possible when working in clay, compared with other sculpture media such as stone, wood or bronze, make clay particularly appealing to the teacher with limited classroom hours as well as to the individual craftsman whose time is at a premium. Furthermore, the fact that the sculpture is built directly in clay, which is then fired to form the finished product, accelerates the learning process and gives a spontaneity and vigor to the end result.

HISTORY

Clay has been used since the beginnings of civilization. The Egyptians invented the brilliant blue ceramic material called "Egyptian Paste," from which they made small ceremonial sculptures, and used clay extensively for the tiny figures they buried with their dead. The ancient Chinese were also very skillful in their use of clay as a medium for pottery and sculpture. Particularly well known are their fine sculptures of horses, many of which have been found in tombs, perfectly preserved through the centuries. The early cultures which sprang up along the shores and on the islands of the Mediterranean produced vigorous, spirited examples of ceramic sculpture as well. In the Western Hemisphere some of

Statuette of a falcon. Egyptian (Old Kingdom)
Glazed ceramic sculpture
Collection: R. H. Lowie Museum of Anthropology, University of Calif.
Photograph, Burton Frasher, Jr.

the most imaginative clay sculptures of all times were created by the Pre-Columbian civilizations of South and Central America. These latter have had a marked influence on the art of our time.

SCOPE

Because working in clay can be exasperating to the beginner if he tries too advanced a design at first, it is best to start with a simple project which can be completed in an hour or two and proceed gradually to the more complex ones. This book is designed to take the beginner through a series of clay sculptures which will gradually build up his knowledge of the medium and teach him how to handle it. To supplement the actual construction, a background of technical information will also be provided to insure the professional quality of the result. With each successful experience, control of the medium and excitement at its possibilities will increase. With the growth of technical skill, the sculptor will adapt his design ideas more inventively to working in clay.

The text covers the simple tools needed, suitable clays and their preparation, ideas and handling of design for ceramic sculpture, a series of projects in construction accompanied by step-by-step photographs, special group projects suitable for a whole class, firing procedures and finishes of various kinds.

When the techniques described in this book have been mastered, the reader should have a very professional grasp of the medium and should be able to execute a great variety of designs. Pursuing this art form still farther will lead him with ever-increasing confidence toward an even more masterful expression of his ideas. Indeed, it would take several lifetimes to explore all of the exciting combinations of subject matter, design, color, and texture which are possible in ceramic sculpture.

Female head. Etruscan
Terra cotta
Collection: R. H. Lowie Museum of
Anthropology, University of Calif.
Photograph, Burton Frasher, Jr.

Musicians. Chinese
Glazed clay, 8-10 inches high
Collection: Honolulu Academy of Arts
Photograph, Burton Frasher, Jr.

Llama. Peruvian
Terra cotta with slip decoration, about
10 inches long
Collection: R. H. Lowie Museum of
Anthropology, University of Calif.
Photograph, Burton Frasher, Jr.

Seated dog. State of Colima, Mexico.
Tarascan culture (3rd century, A.D.)
Burnished terra cotta, about 18 inches
high
Courtesy: Stuart Galleries, Los Angeles,
Calif.
Photograph, the author

Seated figures. Ameca Valley, State of
Jalisco, Mexico. Tarascan culture (5th
century, A.D.)
Terra cotta, about 16 inches high
Courtesy: Stendahl Galleries, Los
Angeles, Calif.
Photograph, the author

T'ang horse. Chinese (618-906 A.D.)
Terra cotta, about 12 inches high
Collection: Mr. and Mrs. William Dieterle,
Hollywood, Calif.
Photograph, Burton Frasher, Jr.

Cock. Etruscan
Terra cotta, 9 inches high
Collection: R. H. Lowie Museum of
Anthropology, University of Calif.
Photograph, Burton Frasher, Jr.

1
Tools

The basic tools needed by the beginner in ceramic sculpture are very simple (Fig. 1). First he will need a square of heavy (10-mil weight) clear plastic sheeting, about 36 by 36 inches, which can be spread out on work table or desk. The sculpture is modeled directly on this sheeting, which protects the surface beneath; the corners of the plastic sheet can be folded over the sculpture to keep it from drying out between work periods. Plastic bags of all sizes are also very useful to slip over the sculpture to prevent drying or to cover part of the structure while another part is either being worked on or drying before the next addition of clay. For covering larger sculptures, plastic drop sheets or appliance covers can be purchased. Plastic used to cover the sculpture can be much lighter than that utilized as a work surface; 1½- to 2-mil thickness is adequate.

If the sculpture must be moved at the end of each session, it is wise to have a work board. A ¾-inch plywood scrap board, about 12 by 16 inches, shellacked or varnished, will serve this purpose very well. It can be slipped under the plastic sheet, or inside several layers of plastic bags, to protect it from moisture. If the board is placed on a thick, folded section of newspaper, it can be turned at will on the work area, permitting the sculptor to view his work from different angles. Sculpture stands are handy if space and budget permit. However, these are not essential, since a table or sturdy wooden box will support the work quite adequately.

A one-pint size, wide-mouthed glass jar for water and a small sponge are necessary while working. Although

Figure 1: *Tools* (left to right): *water bottle, sponge, wire tool, paring knife, spatula, plastic texture tool, dental tool for scoring clay, wooden modeling tool, spray bottle, spoon, stamp with initials, sculpture board, plastic sheet for covering sculpture.*

cellulose sponges cut into 1½-inch squares will serve, natural sponges of fine-grained texture, cut into several pieces, will last considerably longer. An empty window glass cleaner bottle with attached spray nozzle is very useful for spraying a fine mist of water over the sculpture to keep its surface moist and workable. A small flit gun with glass bottle water container will also serve the purpose.

For actual modeling, a metal scratch tool is necessary for scoring the clay in preparation for joining additional clay. A 4- or 5-inch spike or finishing nail, a section of ⅛-inch steel or brass welding rod sharpened at the end, a nut pick or an old dental tool will do the job admirably.

A steel spatula can be used for scoring and for cutting and shaping as well. However, a paring knife is sufficient for all necessary cutting and costs less. Some sort of wire tool should also be obtained for shaping clay, hollowing out solid sculptures and general finishing. Most useful is the type with a round-toothed wire tip at one end and a larger triangular-toothed tip at the other (as illustrated). It should be 10 to 12 inches long. The teeth cut into the wire are excellent for texturing the surface of the sculpture. Spatulas and wire tools are carried by most art stores and art supply houses.

A kitchen spoon is useful for burnishing surfaces and hollowing out sculptures. Other texture tools may be made with a pocket knife. Sucker sticks, tongue depressors, or fragments of hardwood such as maple or ash may be carved with fine or coarsely notched ends which will give a fascinating array of textures to the surface of a sculpture. Little bits of clay may be fashioned into interesting shapes, fired, and used as tools for stamping allover patterns into the clay (Figs. 2 and 3). These may be made in the form of stamps or wheels which can be rolled across the clay, leaving a continuous imprint. Many allover textures can be made with simple, everyday objects such as spoons, nails, screws, nuts and bolts, or a section of a saw blade. The sculptor's initials may be carved in reverse into a clay chunk, which is then fired and makes a very professional signature to stamp upon his work. One of each of the aforementioned tools is all that is necessary for the beginning ceramic sculptor. Later, a wider selection of wire and wooden modeling tools can be added.

Figures 2, 3: *Clay slabs with texture tools showing pattern made by each.*

2
Clay

KINDS OF CLAY

It is important to obtain clay which can be worked easily and which will hold its shape well without sagging or cracking. Fire clays and stoneware clays have been refined to remove organic debris and impurities, and will stand quite high temperatures. Stoneware clay is usually more plastic than fire clay (and often denser and more vitrified after firing), but both make excellent sculpture clays. A few examples of both types are Jordan Stoneware Clay, Zanesville Stoneware, Ohio Fire Clay, Lincoln Fire Clay, and Grefco Fire Clay.

Ball clays are very pliant and sticky. Small amounts of this type may be added to a fire clay mixture, if necessary, to improve its workability. Bentonite is an exceedingly workable ball clay, often added in small amounts to fire clay to achieve greater plasticity or better fit in a glaze formula. It is so plastic that not over 3 per cent need be added to the clay batch.

Earthenware clay can be used for ceramic sculpture but should not be fired to high temperatures because of the metal oxides or fluxes which it contains.

Finely crushed grog—20-mesh to fine-mesh is best—is a necessary addition to all sculpture clay mixtures. Grog is made of finely crushed fire brick and is added to clay to give it porosity, so that during firing the moisture present in the clay can escape; otherwise, it is trapped inside and may cause explosions.

SOURCES OF SUPPLY

There are a number of sources from which clays suitable for ceramic sculpture may be obtained. If space or facilities for mixing batches of clay are lacking, the clay can be obtained ready-mixed with grog, coloring ingredients, and water. The ready-mix clay should have a minimum of 10 per cent, but no more than 30 per cent, grog to insure safe firing. Ready-mix clay usually comes packed in 25- 50-lb. chunks, encased in a plastic bag in which it will stay moist and ready for use for many weeks. Earthenware, stoneware or red architectural clay can be purchased in this form from many ceramic supply houses and local art stores throughout the United States.

In almost every major city there are supply houses which sell materials to the commercial ceramic industries or local pottery plants. These should be able to supply good stoneware or fire clay in powdered form. Sometimes plastic fire clay may be obtained at a local builder's supply, where it is stocked for use by masons and plasterers. Finely crushed grog can be obtained from ceramic supply houses or firebrick manufacturers. Regular brick factories will sometimes sell brick dust, which serves as grog and is less expensive than the finer variety.

MIXING

Mixing clay is a simple, though dusty, procedure. To a large mixing container, add half the dry clay, grog, and coloring oxides, if any are used, and blend the dry mixtures thoroughly by hand or with a paddle. Then add the remainder of the ingredients and dry-mix again. Next, prepare the liquid to be added, which should be in the ratio of ¾ cup of distilled vinegar (which will improve the work-ability of the clay) to about 5 gallons of water per 100 pounds of dry material. Pour this on top of the clay and allow it to stand overnight. By the next morning it will be possible to knead handfulls of the clay to a firm consistency and store an adequate amount in plastic bags, so it is ready when needed.

Another mixing method, if plaster drying slabs are available, is first to blend the dry clay recipe and then add it gradually to a container half-full of water. The mixture is allowed to stand until the water has soaked through the clay. Then it is stirred to remove lumps, and poured onto plaster slabs. It is allowed to dry until the clay blob can be lifted intact from the plaster and is not sticky to the touch. The clay is then stored in covered refuse containers. Great care should be taken not to get chips of plaster in the clay, because any plaster fragment will burst during firing, leaving a little crater.

A bathroom scale may be used to weigh the ingredients in large batches of clay. For more delicate measurements a gram scale is needed.

Before mixing a large batch of sculpture clay, a small amount of a particular formula should be tried out to test its workability. If the clay does not hold its shape well, seems sandy, or cracks easily when a moist coil is twisted, it may lack plasticity. Either 1 per cent bentonite or 10 per cent ball clay may be added to improve its performance. Kentucky or Tennessee ball clays work especially well for this purpose.

If the sculpture clay mixture fires white or buff and a little more color is desired, burnt umber or iron oxide may be added to the dry ingredients before water is added. For a cone 04 firing, add 6 to 7 per cent umber or iron oxide; for a cone 5 firing, add 4 to 5 per cent; and for cones 8 to 10, only 2 to 3 per cent of these ingredients. If the oxides are lumpy they can be run through a 40-mesh screen to assure even color throughout the batch.

FIRING

The term "cone" refers to the temperature to which the clay is fired. This temperature may be measured with a pyrometer (a high temperature measuring device) or a pyrometric cone, which is an elongated, pyramid-shaped piece of clay about three inches tall. Pyrometric cones are compounded of different ingredients which melt at specific temperatures. These cones are better indicators of conditions within a kiln than is a pyrometer. Because the cones quite accurately indicate the effect of both the temperature and the duration of firing, they may fall slightly before the actual cone temperature is reached. The temperatures at which cones melt run from cone 022 (1085° F.) to cone 42 (3659° F.). Thus, to fire a given temperature, a cone is chosen which melts at that temperature. This cone, and two others which melt at slightly lower temperatures, are stuck in a plat of clay, tilted slightly in the direction in which they are expected to fall, and placed on a shelf or post just inside the peephole of the kiln (Fig. 4). For instance, if the kiln is to be fired to cone 5, a No. 5, a No. 4, and a No. 3 cone are placed in a row in the plat of clay with all the cones leaning slightly toward the No. 3 cone, which will fall first. As the No. 3 cone melts, it will fall away from the other cones because it is tilting in that direction. The No. 4 cone will fall next toward cone No. 3, and No. 5 cone will fall last of all, indicating that

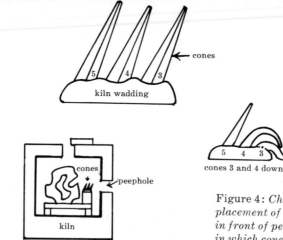

Figure 4: *Chart showing correct placement of cones in plat of kiln wadding in front of peephole in kiln, and manner in which cones melt during firing.*

the kiln should be turned off.

The terms "oxidation" and "reduction" are sometimes confusing, but it is necessary to understand both in order to compound clay bodies and to control the firing. A ceramic sculpture may be fired entirely by oxidation or by a combined oxidation-reduction technique. The oxidation-reduction technique can be used only in kilns fueled by gas, oil, or wood. To oxidize, adjust the burner until the flame is bluish. This means that the flame is given plenty of oxygen and is kept clean and free of carbon. When the maximum temperature desired has almost been reached, adjust the burners to get an orange flame. This will produce a smoky atmosphere within the kiln.

Since the heat in an electric kiln is provided by electricity, the atmosphere is always oxidizing. Some ceramists introduce combustible material into an electric kiln to produce a smoky atmosphere. This, however, eventually causes the electric elements to burn out. Reduction takes place when free carbon and carbon monoxide consume oxygen from the clay or glaze of the ware within.

The following clay mixtures will work well, at low fire or stoneware temperatures, for well-known commercial fire and stoneware clays (available throughout the United States). However, any good local fire clay may be used if the types listed are not obtainable. Suggested fire and stoneware clays which possess good plasticity-porosity ratios are Jordan Stoneware Clay, Lincoln Fire Clay, Zanesville Stoneware Clay, Ohio Fire Clay, and Grefco Fire Clay.

Using grog and clay only:

		Per cent
A. Fire or stoneware clay	. . . .	80
Grog—20-mesh	. . . .	20
(for large sculpture of 1- to 1½-inch wall thickness)		
B. Fire or stoneware clay	. . . .	85
Grog—20-mesh	. . . .	15
(for sculpture of ½- to ¾-inch wall thickness)		

For color, add 1 to 3 per cent red or black iron oxide or 2 to 5 per cent natural red clay.

For texture, add 5 per cent 20-mesh builder's sand, iron sand, 40-mesh ilmenite or 40-mesh iron filings. Test the clay by twisting a moist coil. If it seems too sandy and cracks, ball clay or a little bentonite will improve its plasticity.

		Per cent
C. Fire or stoneware clay	. . . . .	75
Ball clay	. . . .	10
Grog—20-mesh	. . . .	15

D. Fire or stoneware clay 80
Bentonite 5
Grog—20-mesh 15

If the clay seems too plastic, is very sticky, shrinks excessively, and cracks during drying and firing, silica and feldspar may be added. Silica acts as a nonplastic filler and hardens the body. Feldspar at high temperatures acts as a flux, thereby increasing the clay's body density.

	Per cent
E. Fire or stoneware clay	68
Feldspar	10
Silica	7
Grog—20-mesh	15
F. Fire or stoneware clay	65
Feldspar	10
Silica	8
Grog—20-mesh	12
Builder's sand—20-mesh	5

For reduction, red architectural terra cottas give russet brown to black effects and have good characteristics as sculpture clays. Good suggested clay mixes for reduction are as follows:

	Per cent
G. Fire or stoneware clay	50
Natural red clay	20
Silica	5
Feldspar	10
Grog—20-mesh	15
H. Fire or stoneware clay	60
Ball clay	10
Silica	10
Feldspar	10
Grog—20-mesh	10

For black fleck, add 5 per cent 40-mesh builder's sand, iron sand, or 80-mesh ilmenite or iron filings. NOTE: Grog referred to in these formulas is 20- to

fine-mesh, so that all the materials that will go through a 20-mesh screen are included, from powder to 20-mesh particle size. This kind of grog produces the best kind of porosity in a sculpture clay body.

These clays can be fired from cone 05 to cone 10. At lower temperatures they will give a porous, earthenwarelike body, and at higher heat they will show various degrees of densification.

COLOR

In general, the colors obtained in reduction firing are more muted and earthy than those achieved in oxidation, though there is great variation possible with both types of firing. Sculpture can be reduced very successfully, and with a little testing a clay body can be especially compounded to give just the right color and texture at a given temperature and with a given amount of reduction.

Usually, light-colored fire and stone-ware clays, such as Lincoln Fire Clay or Jordan Stoneware, will turn buff or light tan when fired in oxidation and will be dark buff to tan with metallic flecks when fired in reduction.

Many red architectural terra cottas will fire in oxidation to pinkish orange at cone 04, bright orange at cone 5, and tan at cones 8 to 10. In reduction, through the same temperature range, their color will vary from red-brown to chocolate with metallic flecks.

To darken a stoneware or fire clay, 1 to 3 per cent of one of the oxides of iron, or from 2 to 5 per cent of a natural red clay, may be added. These additions will give colors in the medium tan to brown range. To give the clay a grayish cast, 3 to 7 per cent feldspar may be added. Feldspar causes the clay to vitrify and become denser and stronger in the firing. The addition of 5 per cent builder's sand, put

through a 20-mesh screen, will increase the brown and black flecks in both oxidation and reduction.

In addition to the oxides of iron which have already been mentioned, there are others which will give varying shades of earth colors in the tan, red, brown, chocolate-brown, and black range. Shades of yellow, yellow-brown, gray, and dark gray may be obtained with body stains. Some of these additional coloring ingredients are raw and burnt umber, sienna, raw sienna, yellow ochre, manganese carbonate, manganese dioxide, iron chromate, and chrome oxide. The black oxide of iron, manganese dioxide, and to a certain extent the chrome oxide will produce fine flecks throughout the clay body. Colors in the yellow, blue, blue-green, and green range are obtained by using clay body stains prepared from vanadium, cobalt, and copper.

These stains and oxides are expensive, especially in the amounts needed to produce very dark colors in oxidation. They are also strong fluxes which if used in excess can weaken a clay body and at high temperatures can cause it to crack or slump. An alternate method of obtaining color is to use it on the surface only. A small batch of color and clay body without the grog can be mixed and painted on the sculpture as an engobe, or with the addition of grog can be modeled right on the final finished surface. The base clay and grog mix should be the same as that used to build the sculpture, so the shrinkage will be the same. When a large percentage of flux is used for dark colors, the grog content in the color coat can sometimes be slightly higher than that of the base clay. The flux will cause the color coat to shrink more than the clay body so extra grog is added to cut down this shrinkage a little. Color coat formulas and their application will be discussed further in Chapter 7.

3
Design

WHERE TO LOOK FOR IDEAS

Sculpture design can often find its source in some area of nature with which the beginner is already familiar—pets he has studied, the human form, plant or tree shapes; there are multitudes of ideas all around us. Nature films are a marvelous source of fresh, spontaneous subject matter. By seeing the countless varieties of creatures alive in their natural habitats, the sculptor perceives the total dynamic form, not just its isolated parts. This kind of vision promotes creative thinking.

A sketching trip to the local zoo, pet shop, or to a farm is an excellent beginning. A natural history museum can also be of great interest as a source of inspiration. There is a surprising number of books about all phases of life on our planet, richly documented with color pictures, available in libraries or book stores. These books are not only stimulating but are invaluable as reference material (see Appendix III).

If natural forms are chosen as subject matter, it is also helpful to study illustrations of the skeletal and muscular formation of the various plants and animals to develop a basic understanding of the structural similarities of all living things. Studies of seed pods, flowers, and root systems often turn up shapes to delight the evolving sculptor.

STYLE

The stylistic treatment of subject matter can be infinitely varied. Natural forms may be simplified to emphasize the unity of the composition. Bizarre characteristics of the subject may be accentuated, sometimes to the point of caricature. Abstract forms may be combined in many ways to create vital, expressive sculptures.

A helpful exercise in design at this stage is to choose a particular subject from nature and experiment with how many different ways it can be treated in clay. Treat it as a simple pinch sculpture squeezed into shape with fingers only; as a shape to which pieces of clay are attached in patterns; as a solid shape into which textures are cut or pressed with objects at hand such as nut and bolt, nailhead, sucker stick, or rough piece of bark. Sea creatures and insects make good subjects, and the possibilities are endless (Figs. 5 through 7). These little studies give practice working with clay, and many ideas are suggested by the accidental forms which evolve as the clay is squeezed and shaped.

Another helpful exercise is to choose a subject to be modeled at small size

Figures 5, 6, 7: *Variations on a theme: insects, horned toad, crabs, fish.*

Figure 8: *Drawing of human figures.*

Figure 9: (top left) *Largely realistic sculptural treatment of woman.*
(top right) *More abstract treatment of woman.* (lower left)
Abstract treatment of human form. (lower right) *Pure form, no subject matter.*

suggested in Chapter 1 can be made in clay and fired (see Fig. 20). These tools may be used in hundreds of different ways for spontaneous, crisp textural treatments.

Translating emotions into form can be an intriguing problem. Studies in clay can attempt, by the combinations of forms used, to convey states of mind such as anger or tranquility, fear or trust, generosity or greed, protection or rejection, happiness or grief. These exercises provide practice translating ideas into a three-dimensional medium and encourage an experimental approach to the handling of form.

The sculptor may now choose his most promising concept from among his experiments. He should consider its possibilities as a full-fledged piece of ceramic sculpture and perfect it further. It may require simplification or better arrangement of the forms. One or two more carefully modeled studies can be made and in these the problems of support and distribution of masses within the composition brought to their final solution. Changes are difficult to make during the building of a larger sculpture, so all experimentation should be done at this small size (Figs. 21 and 22). These little sketches in clay need be no larger than five inches high and may be made solid. They may be laid up in loops and arches for open grille-like designs, taking care that all parts are well supported. A lump of clay or a pencil may be used as a temporary prop for parts that need to dry a bit before they can stand alone. These little sketches should be saved. Not only are they a record of evolving ideas but they can be used as models for the building of larger sculptures and can serve as tests for the glazes, engobes, or patina finishes which will be used on subsequent works.

with as much realism as possible. The same subject can then be modeled with more simplified forms. Next, it may be modeled in a form which only vaguely suggests the original subject, and finally it should be treated as a series of pure forms which have no recognizable subject matter at all. Figures 8 through 19 show four sequences of this kind, from the first rough drawing from life, through realistic and abstract forms, to pure

forms without discernable subject matter.

While working with these stylistic treatments the beginner can experiment first with single elements, then with two or more repetitive elements of the same or different sizes. An exercise in contrast is helpful. Large solid shapes can be used in conjunction with smaller open forms. Smooth polished forms played against areas rich in texture create exciting effects. The fantastic texture tools

Figure 10: *Drawing of owls.*

Figure 12: *Drawing of a pine tree.*

Figure 11: (top left) *Realistic treatment of owls.* (center top) *Abstract treatment of owls.* (top right and bottom left) *Forms which only vaguely suggest the shapes of owls.* (bottom center and bottom right) *Pure forms with no subject matter.*

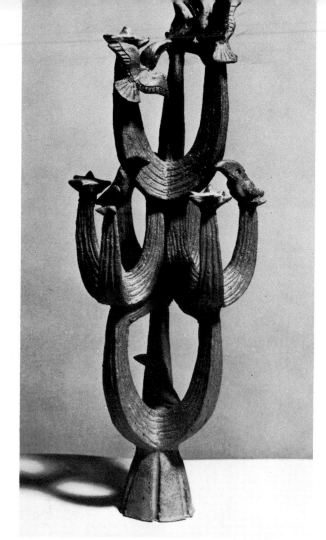

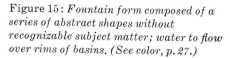

Figure 13: *Fountain suggesting tree form; water to spray upward from flower forms. (See color, p. 27.)*

Figure 14: *Abstract fountain form derived from tree; water to spill over edges of branch forms. (See color, p. 27.)*

Figure 15: *Fountain form composed of a series of abstract shapes without recognizable subject matter; water to flow over rims of basins. (See color, p. 27.)*

Figure 16: *Drawing of gibbons.*

Figure 17: *Studies of gibbons derived from drawing.*

Figure 18: *Semiabstract studies of gibbons.*

Figure 19: *Flying shapes. Idea is developed by working with gibbon forms, but sculpture is a series of pure forms with no subject matter.*

Figure 20: *Texture tools carved in clay and fired. Slab of clay demonstrates resulting patterns.*

Figures 21 and 22: *Developmental stages in the creation of a ceramic sculpture. Small clay studies lead to two different treatments of the same theme—Jonah and the Whale.*

4
Construction

MODELING CLAY SKETCHES
The student may feel himself to be all thumbs when he starts his first small clay study. Practice will, however, quickly improve his touch. In a sketch such as the fountain study (Figs. 23 through 29), all the parts may be made separately and then assembled piece by piece; or they can be formed in place and refined as the structure advances. Each new addition is securely joined by scoring both parts with a scratch tool, moistening each part with a wet sponge, and pressing the parts firmly together. The two parts can then be further worked together with a tool which presses a little soft clay into the joint. Short drying periods are usually necessary between each addition, allowing the clay to stiffen so it will not be deformed during the next addition. The study may be burnished by rubbing with a spoon, or texture may be created with a wire tool. Making these models is often the most purely creative part in the production of a ceramic sculpture, since it is at this stage that the idea first takes three-dimensional form.

Figure 23: *Shaping base and lower branch in construction of small clay sketch.*

Figure 24: *Next branch form is added to structure.*

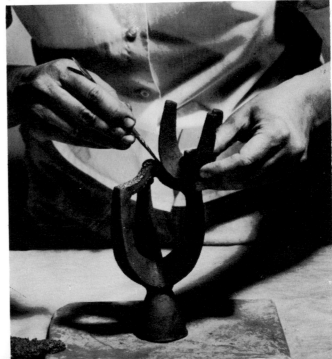

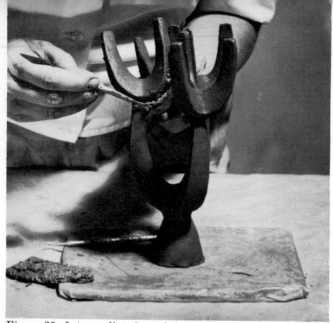

Figure 25: *Intermediate branch forms are in place. Soft clay is worked into joint for strength.*

Figure 27: *Tree form is textured with small wire tool.*

Above: *Fountain Studies (tallest 11″ high). Terra cotta, fired to cone 5— reduced.* Center: *Golden Leopard (39″ long). Terra cotta using coil method with applied textures of golden brown clay. Fired to cone 5—reduced.* Below: *Armadillo (12″ high). Slab method. Glazed and fired in oxidation to cone 9.* Right: *Owls on a Tree (6′4″ tall). Terra cotta, coil method. Glazed and fired in oxidation to cone 9.*

Figure 26: *Upper branch form is fitted into position. Tree is leather-hard now and easily supports weight of branches.*

Figure 28: *Birds and flowers are added to tree.*

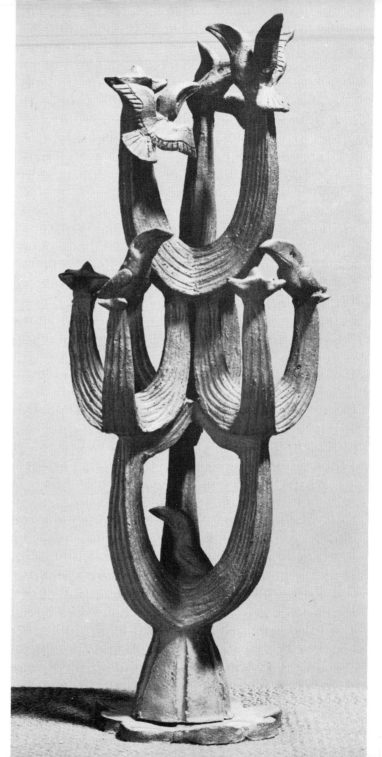

Figure 29: *Finished piece. (See color, p. 27.)*

USE OF THE PAPER CORE

Building a clay sculpture over a paper core is a useful technique for the beginning student (Figs. 30 through 38). Its main advantage is that the whole form may be pressed into shape around the paper core in a relatively short time, and the modeling may proceed without the drying periods required by other methods. It is recommended that only rather small sculptures be built by this method since it is sometimes hard to maintain a consistent wall thickness in large pieces.

A board with a wooden dowel or a metal rod inserted in the center is the basic support for the paper core. A small plastic bag can be fitted over the board. Then twisted newspaper coils are wrapped around the dowel and Scotch-taped into place. The clay is formed around the paper core. Modeling of the forms may follow immediately. Since clay may be quite soft, it needs only scoring before new clay is added. Further wetting might make the area too sticky. When the figure is finished it should be allowed to reach a leather-dry consistency—so that handling will not mar its surface—and then simply lifted off the dowel. The newspaper core can be pulled out through the bottom, leaving a hollow interior, or left to burn out during the early stages of the firing. If the clay completely encloses the paper core, a small vent hole must be punched in the bottom while the sculpture is still damp to let out the gases formed during the firing. Because newspaper compresses easily, the clay will not crack as it shrinks down upon the newspaper while drying. The one disadvantage of this method is that sometimes during the modeling the sculpture wall may become too thick or too thin. Although this is not serious in a small piece, it might prove disastrous in a large one.

Figure 30: *Plastic is taped in place over board with dowel inserted in center. Tiny clay sketch is at right.*

Figure 31: *Twisted newspaper coils are wrapped around dowel.*

Figure 32: *Twisted newspaper has been taped in place. Clay is pressed into position around newspaper.*

Figure 33: *Clay is pressed around newspaper shape. Wall is about ½ inch thick.*

Figure 34: *Clay is closed at top.*

Figure 35: *Forms are modeled on clay shape. Clay was scored before new addition.*

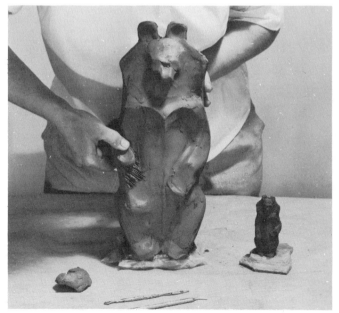

Figure 36: *Bear is roughed out to final size and shape.*

Figure 37: *Forms are finished. Final texture is applied to sculpture; in this case small bits of clay are worked into the surface with a wooden tool.*

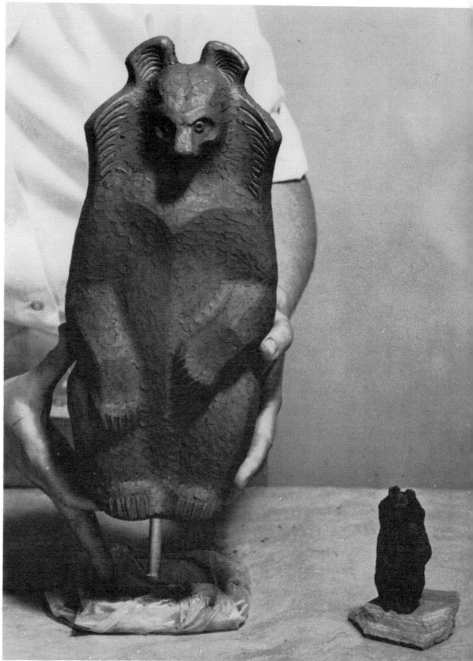

Figure 38: *Finished sculpture is lifted off dowel for drying.*

SOLID SCULPTURES HOLLOWED FOR FIRING

Clay to be built into a solid sculpture can be used as it comes, wet-mixed from the supplier, or, if hand-mixed, be kneaded in small chunks and then pounded into a solid mass (Figs. 39 through 48). It should be of fairly soft consistency. The general shape can be roughed out by pressing, squeezing, and adding more clay where necessary. Sometimes a block of wood is useful to paddle the soft clay into position. The sculpture should be roughed out to approximately its final shape and dimension and allowed to become firm enough for easy handling. It is then laid on its side on a cushion of small pieces of clay and hollowed out from the bottom to a thickness of approximately ½ inch. It is then placed upright again, and the forms are refined. Texture is applied just before it is set aside to dry.

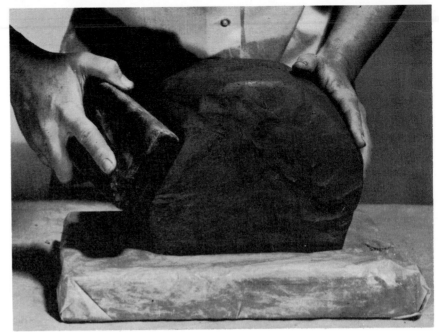

Figure 39: *Solid shape is slapped into position with a wooden block.*

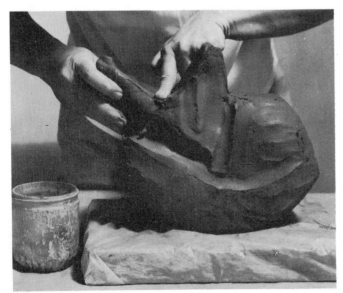

Figure 40: *The forms are roughed out in the soft clay. Pieces of clay are added where necessary.*

Figure 41: *Forms are roughed out to approximate final size and shape.*

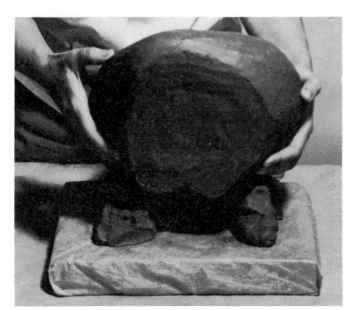

Figure 42: *The sculpture is placed on its side on a pad made of four soft clay lumps.*

Figure 43: *Area to be hollowed out is outlined on clay with a scratch tool.*

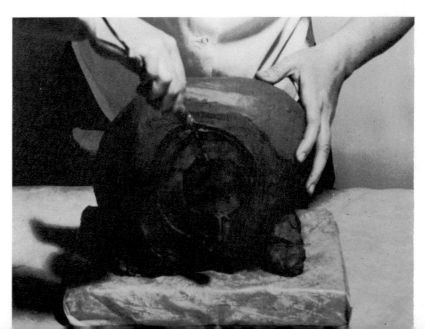

Figure 44: *Sculpture is hollowed out with wire tool.*

Figure 45: *Sculpture wall is thinned to about ½ inch.*

Figure 46. *Sculpture is righted and textured. Texture is being applied with dental tool which has round ball on end.*

Figure 47: *Fine-grained texture is applied with pocket comb.*

Figure 48: *Finished piece.*

If the sculpture is to be a more complex shape that does not lend itself to being hollowed from the bottom, it may be hollowed from the back and the hole covered afterward with a clay wall (see Figs. 49 to 56). The thickness of this new wall should be the same as that throughout the rest of the structure. The clay used for this wall should be of about the same stiffness as the rest of the sculpture, or the new wall may shrink at a different rate during drying, causing cracking. Sculptures should be checked often during drying, because cracks in a still-damp sculpture may be repaired by tamping clay of the same consistency deep down into the crack.

Figure 49: *Monkey sculpture is assembled from solid clay shapes.*
Heavy parts, which were scored and wet, are worked together with the fingers.

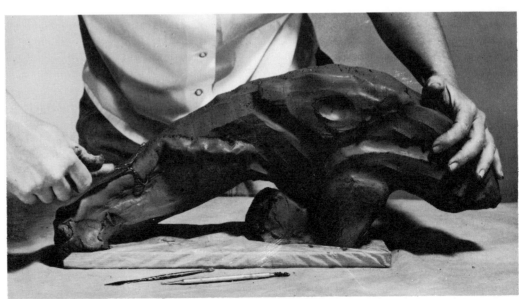

Figure 50: *Forms are roughed in.*

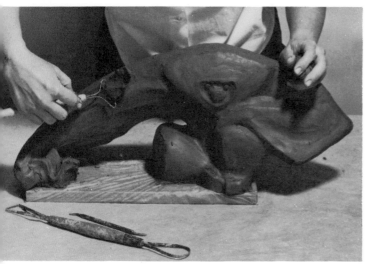

Figure 51: *Monkey is modeled to approximate finished size and shape.*

Figure 52: *Monkey is hollowed out from back. Wall thickness is kept to ½ inch. Wire tool is used for cutting.*

Figure 53: *Edges of hole were scored and wet with a sponge. Clay of the same firmness as the sculpture is used to build back the wall over the opening.*

Figure 54: *Clay wall is rebuilt. New wall should be the same thickness as the rest of the sculpture.*

Figure 55: *When the clay wall is completed the sculpture is refined. Its final texture is achieved with a grooved wire tool.*

Figure 56: *Finished piece.*

A tall, thin shape may be hollowed by cutting the figure in half, hollowing out both parts, and rejoining them (see Figs. 57 through 65). The edges must be well scored and dampened with a sponge before the two halves are put together again. A finger hole may be cut so that the two edges may be rejoined by working the clay together inside as well as outside for a perfect joint. To fill the hole, its edges are first scored and the area dampened with a sponge. Then a chunk of clay of the same consistency is scored, dampened, and pressed into the hole. The forms are then modeled to their final state and the surface given its final texture. All sculptures should be vented with a small hole to prevent the formation of steam pressures during firing.

Figure 57: *Clay is shaped with a block of wood.*

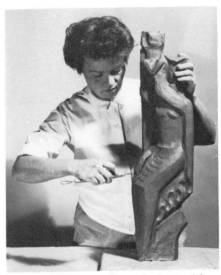

Figure 58: *Forms are roughed out with a wire tool.*

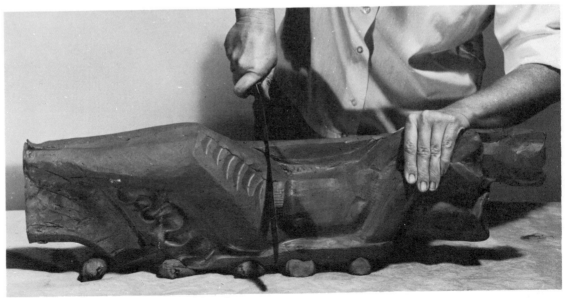

Figure 59: *Sculpture is laid on a cushion of clay balls and cut in half with a knife or cutting wire.*

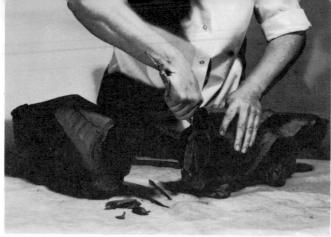

Figure 60: *The two halves are hollowed out, leaving a wall thickness of ½ inch.*

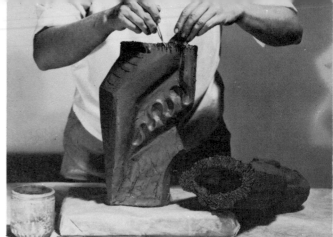

Figure 61: *Lower half of sculpture is set upright. The edges to be joined are scored with a scratch tool and wet with a sponge.*

Figure 62: *The two halves are pressed together.*

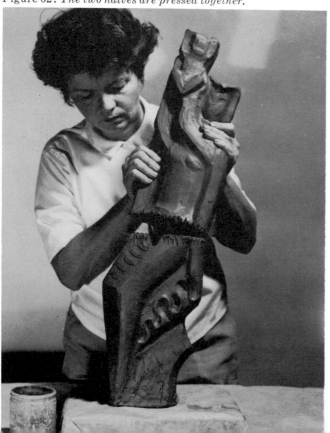

Figure 63: *A hole has been left so a finger can be inserted to join inside as well as outside surfaces for a good bond.*

Figure 64: *Forms have been finished and final texture is applied.*

Figure 65: *Finished piece.*

SLAB BUILDING

The slab method is a free and playful
technique widely used by ceramic
sculptors today (see Figs. 66-72).
The soft clay is rolled out to the desired
thickness with a rolling pin. It can be
rolled out on a plaster or wood surface,
and should be turned occasionally to
prevent sticking. Plaster absorbs water
rapidly, so if it is used for rolling out the
clay then the slab should be moved to
another surface for cutting. The clay can
also be rolled out on newspapers if it is
turned after each pass with the rolling
pin and moved to a dry layer of papers for
cutting. If left too long it causes the
newspapers to become damp, disintegrate,
and stick to the clay. The thickness
of the clay slab depends on the size of the
sculpture to be made. The sculptures
shown here were cut from slabs about
⅜ inch thick. For larger sculptures the
clay can be ¾ to 1 inch in thickness. Paper
patterns should be worked out in
advance and then laid on the slab of clay
and cut out with paring knife or spatula.
The flat clay shape is then pinched
and twisted into the proper form. A short
drying period may be necessary before
the shaping is completed in order that
the figure will support itself without
sagging. Eyes, ears, and other details are
then added, plus whatever refinement of
the edges may be necessary in case
of tears in the clay.

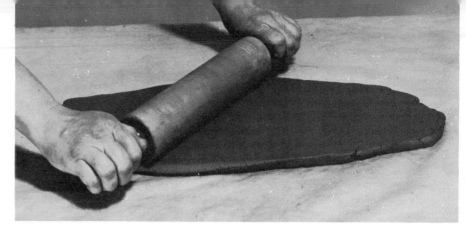

Figure 66: *Clay slab is rolled out with rolling pin ⅜ inch thick.*

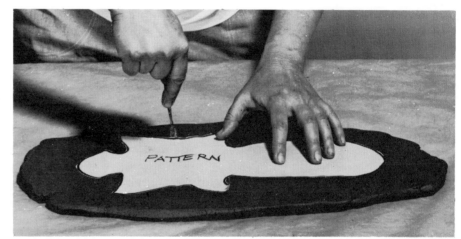

Figure 67: *Paper pattern is placed on slab and design is cut out with knife or spatula.*

Figure 68: *Clay design is lifted carefully.
Head is shaped first.*

Figure 69: *The body is pinched and squeezed into the proper position. A drying period may be necessary before the body will support itself without sagging.*

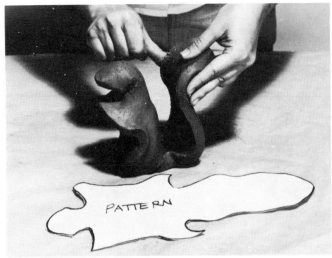

Figure 70: *The tail is lifted and formed.*

Figure 71: *The tail has been attached to the back for support. Eyes have been applied with one of the stamps in the foreground. An ear is attached after the clay has been scored and wet.*

Figure 72: *The squirrel has been refined to improve the curves of tail and body.*

Next a more complex design may be attempted—perhaps a textured animal such as an armadillo (Figs. 73-82). It may be necessary to try several paper patterns before just the right shape is obtained. For a high, rounded form such as this, a clay die can be made over which the armadillo's shell will be shaped. This die can be wrapped tightly in a plastic bag so it will retain its contour and a small piece of cheesecloth or paper towel laid over it so the clay slab will not stick to the plastic. The slab is placed on the die, shaped, textured, allowed to stiffen for easier handling, and then removed. The shell is then laid upside down on a cushion of clay balls, the bottom edges are joined, feet and tail are attached, and the whole is allowed to dry until the feet will support the shell. Then the sculpture is righted and the head, eyes, and ears added.

Figure 73: *Paper pattern for armadillo is removed from cut slab of clay.*

Figure 74: *Slab of clay is laid over shaping form, which is raised on a block of wood so the side tabs will hang free.*

Figure 75: *Clay is pressed into desired shape, and texture is applied with round texture wheel.*

Figure 76: *Additional texture is stamped on with a nut and bolt.*

Figure 77: *Shell is placed upside down on a cushion of clay balls, and the shell is joined in the center.*

Figure 78: *Feet are attached. Head section formed from a slab and textured with a nut and bolt lies at left, tail at right.*

Figure 79: *Armadillo is resting on its feet. Its head is being attached.*

Figure 80: *The eye has been applied, and the ear is joined to head.*

Figure 81: *Armadillo is finished. Edge of ear is refined.*

Figure 82: *Finished piece.*

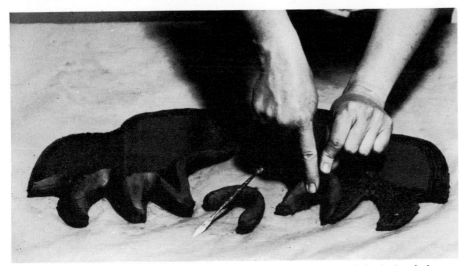

Figure 83: *Left and right facing halves of peccary are laid out, and legs and snout are thickened for better support. Edges have been scored.*

Figure 84: *Slabs are formed in sag box.*

A sculpture may be constructed from two or more slabs of clay (Figs. 83 through 92). A left and a right facing slab are cut from the clay. Then the parts that will support the sculpture later—the feet and snout in the case of the peccary—are built up for extra strength. A spacing web of clay can be added to maintain the proper distance between slabs when they are assembled. Where necessary, edges are scored for joining. Then the slabs are laid in sag boxes or over clay die forms. A sag box can be made by pinning a square of cheesecloth over the edges of a cardboard box. For a shallow curve the cheesecloth can be stretched tight; for a deep curve, it can be left rather loose. The slabs of clay take on dimension in the sag box and are allowed to stiffen slightly before they are assembled. The scored edges are then reworked slightly and wet with a sponge. Next, the slabs are stood on edge and the scored areas squeezed together like the rim of a pie crust. Other parts such as cheek ruffs and ears are cut out, curved in the sag box, and securely attached to the body. Any modeling, texturing, or other refinements are then done.

Figure 85: *After wetting scored edges with a sponge, right and left halves are in position for joining.*

Figure 86: *Edges of the two halves are pressed together like the edge of a pie crust. Structure is stiff enough to support its own weight on legs and snout.*

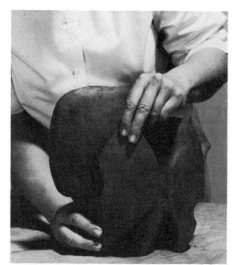

Figure 87: *After cutting and forming in sag box, cheek ruff is fitted to body.*

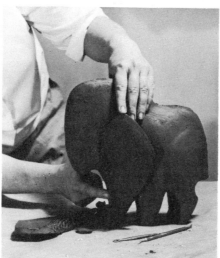

Figure 88: *Cheek ruff has been scored and wet with a sponge and is joined to body. Cheek ruff for other side is at left.*

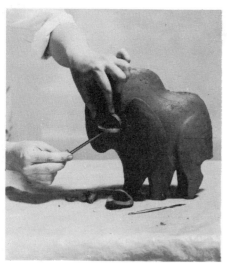

Figure 89: *Ear is added to scored, dampened area.*

Figure 90: *Eyes and tusks have been added and textures are cut where needed.*

Figure 91: *Final allover texturing done with a section of a saw blade.*

Figure 92: *Finished piece.*

Figure 93: *Rolls of clay for base are joined together. Clay sketch is at right.*

Figure 94: *Foot and tail stubs are securely joined to base.*

Figure 95: *First leg arch is added.*

Figure 96: *First leg arch is temporarily supported with stick. Second leg is added.*

SOLID ARCH CONSTRUCTION

An open grille-like sculpture may be built using solid coils of clay connected to each other in a series of arches, each supporting the one above. The clay used for this method should be malleable and contain 15 per cent grog so that the solid section will fire safely. The design must be skillfully handled in this type of composition to ensure that the arches are placed to give adequate support to the upper forms. In the design used in Figures 93 through 104 (see also Frontispiece), the upper cat rests on a branch which goes down to the base on one side and connects to the lower cat's neck on the other. The tail of the upper cat connects also to the neck of the lower cat, which is well supported by its legs, tail, and the lower branch form. If the arches are weak and soft when first laid up into position, they can be supported by a block of wood, a roll of clay, or even a pencil. The support should be removed as soon as the coil will support its own weight. The first arches should be connected as dictated by the design and then allowed to dry to a leather-hard consistency. They can then be modeled somewhat to establish their form and approximate their final size. Then the upper arches may be added one at a time, allowing drying periods where necessary. The lower arches should be covered with a plastic sheet while the upper ones are drying. This prevents

Figure 97: *Tail arch is added. After each arch is joined at both ends it is adjusted and shaped until it has the right direction and height.*

Figure 98: *Body arch is added.*

Figure 99: *Cat's head has been added. Upper branch is added.*

Figure 100: *Upper cat's body arch is added.*

their becoming too dry for later modeling and finishing. Each new arch should be securely attached by scoring and wetting both surfaces to be joined and then working them together, adding soft clay to fill out the joint. After each arch is in place and has stiffened slightly it can be built up in diameter until it approximates its final size. When the whole structure has been built up and is stiff enough to support itself, the forms can be modeled and finished.

Figure 101: *Upper cat's tail is secured.*

Figure 102: *Head is attached.*

Figure 103: *Branch is attached. The structure is now complete and the forms have been roughed into final size.*

Figure 104: *The forms are finished. Bodies of cats are burnished with a spoon to contrast with textured base and branch forms. (See also Frontis piece)*

Figure 105: *Shape of lower edge of portrait is sketched on sculpture board with a marking pencil.*

Figure 106: *First coil is laid down. This coil is slightly thicker than the rest will be.*

Figure 107: *The next-thinner coil is added.*

Figure 108: *The coils are joined well inside and out.*

COIL METHOD

The coil method of building is especially suitable for larger sculptures whose cross sections would be too thick for successful firing. It eliminates the hollowing-out process and makes it easier to control wall thickness (Figs. 105–116). A small model is made first, to establish pose and basic head shape. The size and shape of the bottom edge of the portrait can be drawn on the plastic-covered board and the first coil of clay laid down just inside this line. The first coil must be thicker than the succeeding ones, since it is the main load-bearing surface. On a life-size portrait such as the one shown, the first coil should be ¾ inch thick and the succeeding coils ½ inch thick.

The coils forming the neck should be slightly over ½ inch thick to assure sturdy support for the head. The head coils can be slightly under ½ inch, since more clay will be added during the finishing of the face forms. When the structure is completed the forms may be modeled by scoring and wetting the sculpture and adding soft clay where necessary.

Figure 109: *The shoulders have been roughed in and the neck coil is attached.*

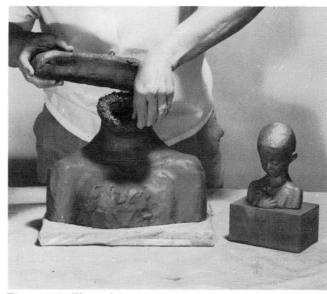

Figure 110: *The neck is completed and the first head coil is added.*

Figure 111: *Next coil is added.*

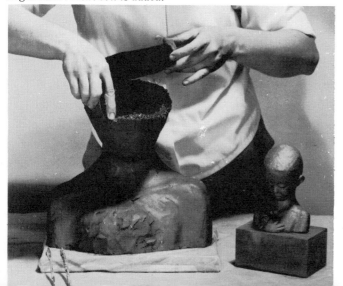

Figure 112: *Head form begins to curve inward.*

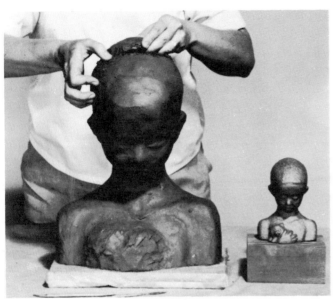

Figure 113: *The head is closed at the top. Face has been roughed in.*

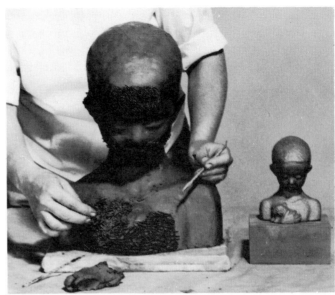

Figure 114: *Portrait is scored with scratch tool and wet with a sponge.*

Figure 115: *Clay is added to build up forms.*

Figure 116: *Finished piece, showing final modeling of surface.*

Sculptors sometimes use proportional calipers as an aid in modeling portraits from life and in enlarging sculptures from smaller models. A set is easy to make (Fig. 117). Two strips of pine wood 1 inch wide, ½ inch thick, and 18 inches long can probably be found in the scrap bin of a school woodshop or local lumberyard. Sharpen all four ends to identical tapering points and lay the strips in a crossed position on a work table. Place a ruler at either end and then open the points so that one end measures 1 inch and the other end 2 inches. Mark each strip at the exact center of the spot where the two boards cross and drill a hole in each strip at that spot. A ¼-inch-diameter bolt about 1¼ inches long, a wing nut to fit it, and two small washers should be used to assemble the calipers. Mark this spot as the 1-to-2 proportion. Now a measurement taken on the sketch with the small end of the calipers will measure twice that size on the large end. The calipers may also be assembled to measure for different proportions. For instance, measure 1 inch on the small end and 3 inches on the large end for a 1-to-3 ratio, or 1 inch on the small end and 4 inches on the large end for a 1-to-4 ratio. Although these calipers can serve as an aid in checking the accuracy of enlargements, the beginner should also try to improve the accuracy of his eye and rely as little as possible upon mechanical aids.

The coil method may also be used for very large sculptures, and the advanced student may want to execute a promising idea to monumental scale. The size of the available kiln for firing his work is the only real limitation. Sometimes a large sculpture may be made in two or more parts which can be fired separately in a smaller kiln and then assembled upon completion. Building the sculpture this way simplifies all stages of the work. The sculpture illustrated in Figures 118

through 137 was designed to divide in the middle. The structure should be started with the thickest coils directly on the sculpture board, since this is the load-bearing surface and will support a great deal of weight in the final stages. The wall is built up as in the portrait by adding successive coils to the scored, dampened rim of the growing wall below. Drying periods are necessary after about every 4 inches of added height. When the point at which the sculpture is to be divided is reached, an inner shaft should be built up from inside the main wall. It should rise 4 to 8 inches and be covered by a strip of plastic. Then the continuation of the main wall is started by laying a coil of clay around the inner shaft, right on the rim of the lower wall section. The plastic will keep the joints from sticking together. This new coil is trimmed to the exact size of the lower tree trunk and then built up past the fork in the branches, at which point it is corrected for size and direction, using the small sketch as a guide. Now the lower section should be finished—modeled, refined, and given its final texture. The partially completed upper trunk is shaped and textured to match and then lifted off onto its own sculpture board. The building is then continued coil by coil; the upper part should be checked against the small sketch from time to time to correct the size and position of the various new additions.

For a somewhat smaller sculpture, all the sections may be left in place during modeling, finishing, and even glazing, separating them only for drying and firing. The owl tree group was glazed, using the same amount of glaze on each half, and both halves were fired side by side in the same kiln. Most schools have access to a small kiln, so that sections can be fired one at a time, taking care to maintain consistent firing conditions each time.

DRYING

The drying of sculpture needs careful attention. Sculptures should be dried gradually, avoiding direct sunlight, excessively warm temperatures, and drafts. To dry it, the sculpture should be uncovered for short periods of time at first, until it begins to lighten in color. Then it should be covered with a dry towel or a piece of cotton sheet to allow further slow drying. Thin parts can be wrapped with a scrap of cloth so they will not dry faster than thicker sections. If cracks appear while the sculpture is still leather-hard, they may be filled by tamping some scrap clay of the same consistency down into the crack with the head of a large finishing nail. When the crack has been tamped full, the surface can be pounded smooth with a little block of wood and then retextured to match the surrounding portions.

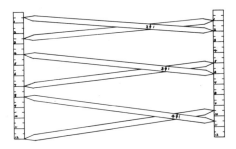

Figure 117: *Chart showing how to make proportional calipers.*

Figure 119: *Root forms are built with ½-inch-thick coils.*

Figure 118: *Beginning of large coil-built sculpture. Position of tree roots has been drawn on sculpture board with marking pencil. First coils laid down are 1 inch thick for extra strength.*

Figure 120: *Root forms have been completed and trunk form is started.*

Figure 121: *Trunk form forks and continues to rise.*

Figure 122: *Owl form is started on the trunk at right and foliage form at left.*

Figure 123: *Soft clay coils are added to the scored, dampened surfaces of the growing sculpture.*

Figure 124: *The upper wing of the owl is built higher. Drying periods occur between additions to allow the structure to stiffen.*

Figure 125: *Lower half of structure is almost completed. Inner shaft of joint is added.*

Figure 126: *The outer part of the upper trunk section has been started and is placed over shaft on lower trunk for accurate fit. Plastic is wrapped around lower shaft to prevent two parts sticking together.*

Figure 127: *New coil is added to upper trunk section.*

Figure 128: *Upper section is built up to fork and trimmed to the exact size of the lower trunk.*

Figure 129: *Lower section has been finished and textured. Upper trunk is textured to match lower trunk.*

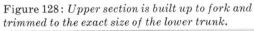

62

Figure 130: *Upper section is lifted off shape and placed on a separate sculpture board.*

Figure 131: *Upper section is scored for next addition of clay.*

Figure 132: *Another coil is added.*

Figure 133: *Owls are started on upper branches.*

Figure 134: *Owls are nearly completed.*

Figure 135: *Owls are completed. Foliage forms are started.*

Figure 136: *Upper section is completed and textured.*

Figure 137: *Owl group completed. Owl tree sculpture was glazed raw, fired to cone 9, and is here shown assembled as planned. (See color page 27.)*

5
Class Projects

This chapter suggests two different large-scale projects which could be undertaken by a whole class. Variations of these two basic ideas may be adapted to fit the working facilities and kiln capacity and might be presented to the school upon completion as a permanent installation.

If the kiln available to the sculpture class is small, a structure can be designed consisting of many sections planned to stack one upon the other. These sections may be fired one at a time if necessary and assembled after firing. There is also the possibility that larger sections could be fired in a local commercial kiln.

FOUNTAIN

For a project such as the one illustrated in Figures 138 through 163, plaster press molds will assure similarity of the parts which, when assembled, will form the basic sections of the fountain. Paper patterns of the sections can be cut out and pinned to the wall to help visualize the finished form. The perfected paper pattern is used as a guide in the modeling of the necessary shapes.

These shapes should be designed so that a simple two-piece mold can be made from them. Draw a line around the sculpture where the mold will divide. Shim stock brass (about .003 gauge) or thin aluminum sheets can be cut up into wedge-shaped pieces 1 by 2 or 3 inches in size and pressed into the clay along the line to form the separation betwen the two halves of the mold.

Plaster is mixed by filling a porcelain, enamel or plastic dishpan about half-full of water and sifting the plaster into it until it rises to the surface of the water. The mixture should be allowed to set for three or four minutes and then stirred with a spoon or stick for two or three minutes to remove lumps and let air bubbles rise to the surface. The clay to be cast should be sprayed with a thin film of water to help prevent air bubbles forming in the mold. The plaster is then poured gradually over the clay form taking care not to trap air bubbles in the corners. Additional coats of plaster are built up on this first layer to a total thickness of about 1 inch and trimmed off at the edges of the metal shim dividers. Then the whole form, plaster mold half and all, is turned over and the process repeated on the other side. The halves of the plaster mold are then separated and dried for a day or two.

A fat roll of clay is pressed into each half of the mold and scooped out down the center, leaving a wall thickness of about ½ inch. The edges of the clay are scored and wet and the two plaster shells with their clay liners pressed together tightly. The clay rims to be joined can protrude ⅛ inch above the edges of the plaster mold so that when the two halves meet they are pressed firmly enough to bond the clay. If the mold is supported by a bed of crushed newspaper, kneeling on it will exert extra pressure.

In a half-hour the clay inside will have shrunk slightly and the plaster shell may be removed. If there are any cracks they may be tamped full of soft clay. The necessary units for the design are pressed and assembled. All parts should be covered with plastic sheets or sacks between working periods so they will remain in good working consistency.

The fitting of the completed sections to the parts upon which they will be stacked is important. They can be tested for fit when in a leather-dry condition. If they fit properly then, they should not change appreciably during firing. Smaller parts such as birds, fish, or flower forms can be attached and fired in place or be fired separately and joined later with cement or epoxy bonding resins. The whole structure can be assembled and the hollow core poured solid with concrete and reinforcing steel, or the sections may be joined with epoxy resin. If epoxy is used, the clay joints should not be glazed, because epoxy holds better on slightly rough surfaces. The nesting of the joints should be very ample and the whole structure stable by itself. Copper tubing of ¼ inch diameter connected to a re-circulating pump may carry water to all parts of the fountain. Valves at the pump can control the height of the water jet.

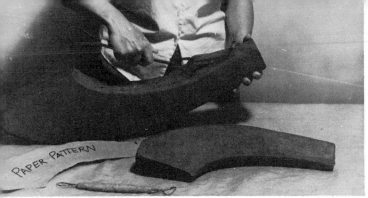

Figure 138: *Branch form for tree fountain is shaped with aid of a paper pattern.*

Figure 139: *No. 003-gauge shim brass is placed in clay to serve as dividers between two halves of plaster molds.*

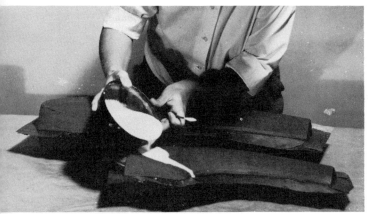

Figure 140: *First thin coat of plaster poured on clay in a continuous stream to avoid trapping bubbles in cracks.*

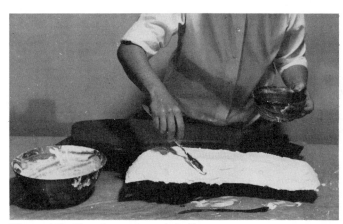

Figure 141: *Top plaster layer is built up to a thickness of 1 inch.*

Figure 142: *First two plaster mold halves have been completed and turned over. Plaster is spread on second halves.*

Figure 143: *Both halves of plaster molds have been completed, separated, and dried. Soft clay is pounded into mold to press first branch form for fountain.*

Figure 144: *Clay is hollowed out to thickness of ½ inch. Edges will then be scored.*

Figure 145: *The edges have been scored and dampened, and the two halves of the mold are pressed together.*

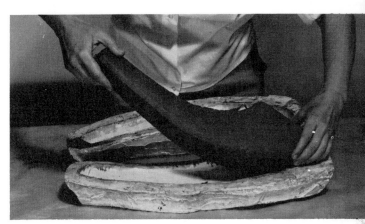

Figure 146: *Mold has been separated. Completed hollow branch form is removed.*

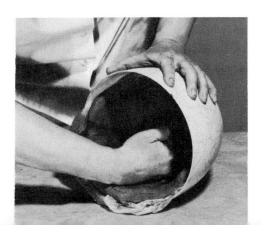

Figure 147: *Base for tree fountain is pressed inside a fiberglas dome shape. A bowl or any other round shape can be used. Line the shape with a layer of Saran wrap or other thin plastic to prevent clay sticking to wall of form.*

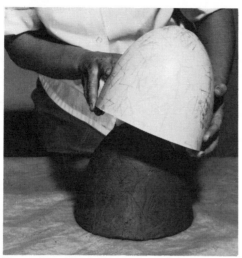

Figure 148: *Fiberglas dome is removed from clay form.*

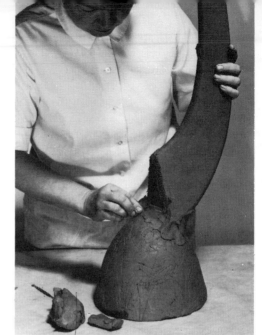

Figure 149: *First branch is attached to base.*

Figure 150: *Third branch is attached to base.*

Figure 151: *First section is completed.*

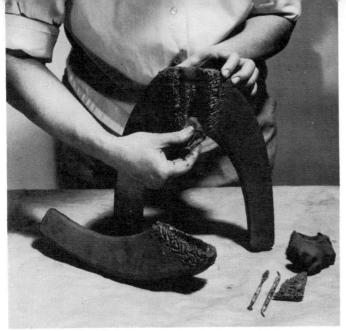

Figure 152: *One of smaller branch units is assembled.*

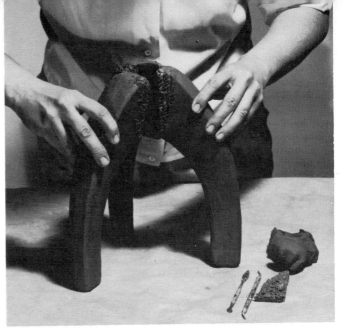

Figure 153: *Smaller branch form is completed.*

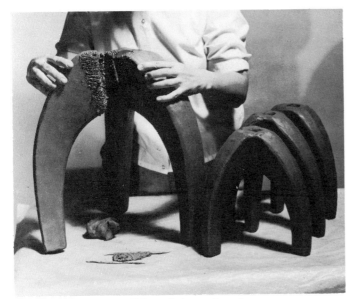

Figure 154: *Three small branch forms have been completed. Upper branch form is assembled.*

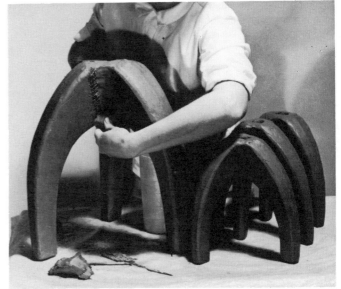

Figure 155: *Upper branch form is completed.*

Figure 156: *Small branch form is fitted to base section.*

Figure 158: *Rich textures are modeled to tree trunk and branches.*

Figure 157: *Small branch forms are fitted to base section.*

Figure 159: *More textures are applied to trunk and branches.*

Figure 161: *Tulip cups from which water will emerge are fitted to tree.*

Figure 160: *Top branch form is fitted in place.*

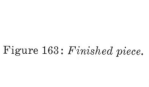

Figure 162: *Brass rod with ceramic birds attached is fitted in place. Brass rod will support the birds just above the water jets which will emerge from the upper tulip cups.*

Figure 163: *Finished piece.*

Figure 163A: *Variation of fountain, using same molds as for Figure 163.*

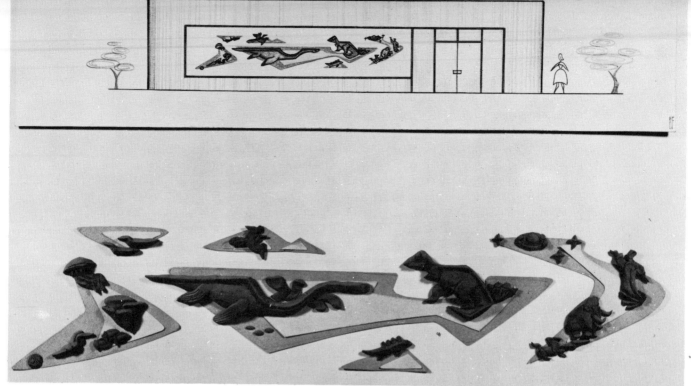

Figure 164. (above) *Scale drawing of proposed mural showing its relation to wall area on building.* (below) *Rough clay sketch for mural done at ¼-inch to 1-foot scale, shown laid out on paper patterns of background color areas. If size permits, full scale paper patterns of the designs may be made and tried on the actual wall to aid in planning.*

MURAL

Another large-scale project that a class might execute is a ceramic wall mural which upon completion might be presented to the school as a permanent decoration for one of its exterior or interior wall areas (Figs. 164-169). The subject might be some aspect of learning— perhaps the history of man, or evolution. The installation site should be chosen early in the planning, since it will determine the size, shape, and to a certain extent the color limitations for the mural. Next, the handling of the main sculptural masses and the large background areas should be worked out. To help clarify the design, paper patterns painted the desired color can be tried in place on the wall, or a one-quarter or one-half inch to the foot scale model may be made. Flat colored areas and sculptured groups can be tried in various combinations until a balanced, pleasing whole emerges.

As the design progresses, thought should be given to what ceramic treatment will be used for the various areas—colors to be used, whether colors are to be glazes or painted on in the form of a colored engobe (mixture of clay and coloring material), which forms will be smooth and which will be richly textured. These are all decisions which should be made before the actual work in clay begins.

The colored areas, if any, behind the sculptured forms may be done in colored stucco or free-form glazed tiles. Clay slabs rolled flat, about ⅜ inch thick, cut to the desired shapes, with the backs incised with horizontal grooves ¼ inch deep, can be used as tiles, either glazed or painted with colored engobes.

The sculptured groups may be from 1 to 2 inches thick. The clay for these groups is rolled out to the right thickness and the shapes cut out with the help of paper patterns, modeled, and textured. If too large to handle easily, they can be cut into smaller sections, each of which should have ¼-inch-deep horizontal grooves cut in the back for setting in mortar on the wall. One way to keep track of the various parts of the mural is to lay them out on a large paper which has a crayon outline of the design drawn upon it. The pieces can even be numbered so the mural will be installed in the proper sequence.

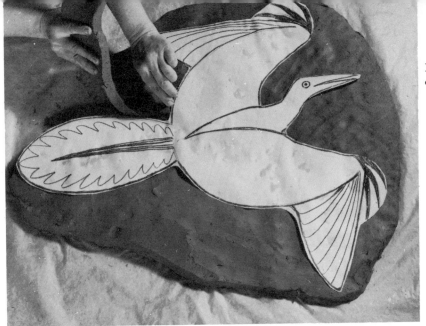

Figure 165: *Paper pattern is laid on clay slab for cutting out sculpture.*

Figure 166: *Modeling the sculpture.*

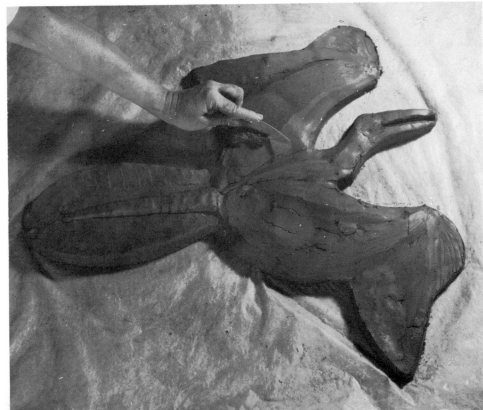

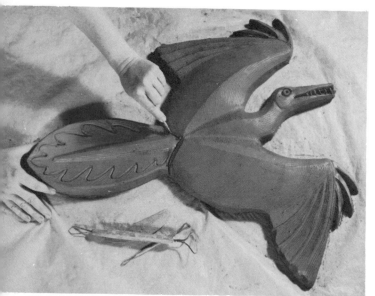

Figure 168: *Horizontal grooves ¼ inch deep are cut into the back of the sculptured parts for a good bond with mortar during later installation. Small cutout clay slabs, as shown, may be glazed or painted with engobe and placed around sculptures for a colored background. Background areas may also be done in colored stucco.*

Figure 167: *After final details and textures have been added, the sculpture is cut into two sections for ease in firing and installation. Larger elements may be cut into more sections as necessary.*

Figure 169: *Sculptured pieces are shown laid out on full scale pattern. These patterns may be used to locate mural elements on the wall as well as to outline colored backgrounds.*

6
Firing Procedures

KILNS

In areas where natural gas is difficult to obtain, kilns can be fired with bottled gas, oil, or electricity. For school and studio use, electricity is a very good source of heat. It is clean, odorless, needs no stack above the kiln for firing, and produces very good results. Glo-bar elements made of silicon carbide are used for reaching temperatures up to cone 19. In electric kilns reduction is not generally recommended.

If the sculptor does not have a kiln, a local artist-potter might be willing to fire work for a reasonable charge. Or the yellow pages of the telephone directory might be consulted for a commercial kiln that will undertake to fire work outside work. Each piece to be transported to the kiln should be packed in a separate cardboard carton on a layer of crushed paper or paper excelsior. The ideal solution of course is to buy or make a kiln. There are many excellent makes on the market (see Appendix II).

On page 80 are general plans for an open-fire updraft (venting out the top) kiln for oxidation or reduction (Figs. 172, 173). If it is intended for school use, this kiln could be made by the students, with teacher supervision, as a class project. Used refractory brick can be bought cheaply and would serve as the basic material. The welding of the angle iron frame might be done in the school or local metal shop, as might be the fabrication of the sheet metal hood and stack. The stack can vent out the roof or out a window. The gas pipe, valves, and burners can be put together

with the aid of a skilled instructor. The brick can be laid using a high-temperature kiln cement for mortar and a hand level for accuracy. The floor slabs and damper pulls should be of refractory material or silicon carbide, purchased from a reputable manufacturer. The shelves should be ⅝- or ⅜-inch-thick silicon carbide—six should be enough.

Pressure gauges or a calibrated valve control would serve equally well for regulating flame intensity. The opening in the kiln can be closed for firing simply by bricking it up with extra brick and stuffing kiln wadding in the cracks. A peephole can be left for viewing the cones during firing. The atmosphere in an open-fire kiln of this type can be kept oxidizing by leaving the damper wide open and the venturi burner air adjuster sufficiently open. For reduction, the damper may be closed part way until flames emerge around the damper opening. The author has used an open-fire updraft kiln similar to this one very successfully for both oxidation and reduction.

Extra refractory brick will serve well as shelf supports in the kiln. Other types which take up less room can also be made by the students. Fire clay with grog used for sculpture clay may be rolled out into a 1½-inch slab, then cut into 1½-inch strips which may in turn be cut into 2-, 4-, 6- or 8-inch post lengths. They can be leveled by setting them up in rows according to height and pressing a flat board gently on their tops. Taller posts can be made by widening the bottoms of the strips for greater stability. These can be fired in the first kiln firing.

A tiny lump of kiln wadding placed on each kiln post will keep the shelf from rocking when it is set on the posts. The shelves should be coated with a layer of kiln wash to make cleaning easier in case glaze drops during firing, as well as to prevent sculptures from sticking to the shelves. Kiln wadding can be a mixture of 1 part fire clay to 1 part fine grog. Kiln wash can be 1 part kaolin to 1 part silica, or 1 part kaolin to 2 parts silica.

FIRING

The firing of ceramic sculpture is a special problem because of the somewhat thicker wall sections and irregular shapes of the pieces. The main hazard to avoid is explosion. This happens when ware is fired too rapidly and the moisture within the piece, instead of slowly working its way through the clay wall and out between the clay particles, builds up inside the walls and forms steam. Steam has great force, and when it forms in sufficient quantities it will explode, blowing the sculpture to bits or popping large pieces right off the sides.

To avoid this the clay used in small sculptures should contain at least 10 per cent 20- to fine-mesh grog and for larger pieces, where the wall thickness is up to 1 inch, should contain 15 per cent grog. It is also important to be sure the ware is thoroughly dry before firing and to have a very slow firing cycle. The most critical period is between 150° F and 212° F, the temperature at which steam forms, and up to 500° F, at which time physically combined water will be dissipated. It is during this early

Figures 170 and 171: *Sculptures loaded on movable floor of very large kiln, ready to be pushed into the firing chamber for firing.*

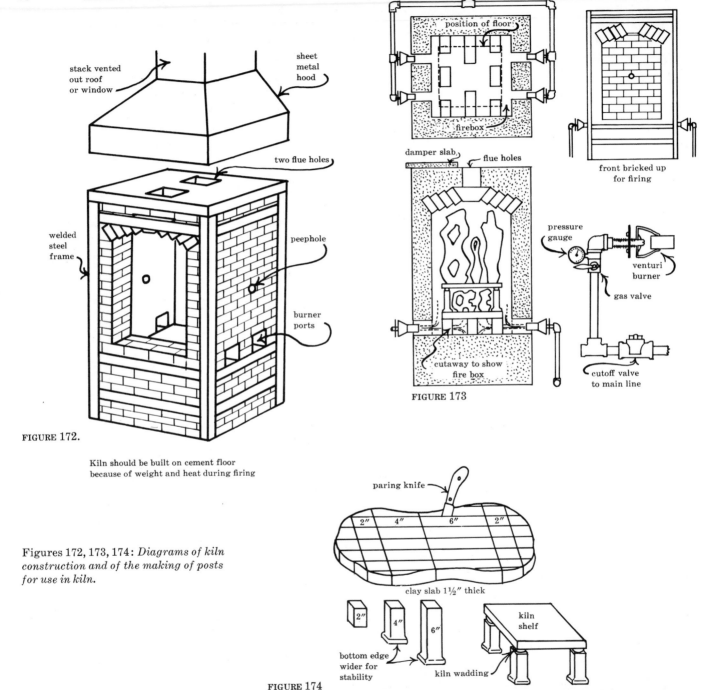

stack vented
out roof
or window

sheet
metal
hood

two flue holes

welded
steel
frame

peephole

burner
ports

FIGURE 172.

Kiln should be built on cement floor
because of weight and heat during firing

position of floor

firebox

front bricked up
for firing

damper slab

flue holes

pressure
gauge

venturi
burner

gas valve

cutaway to show
fire box

cutoff valve
to main line

FIGURE 173

Figures 172, 173, 174: *Diagrams of kiln
construction and of the making of posts
for use in kiln.*

paring knife

2"   4"   6"   2"

clay slab 1½" thick

2"

4"

6"

bottom edge
wider for
stability

kiln
shelf

kiln wadding

FIGURE 174

period that steam explosions can occur.

There should be a heat-soaking period of from six hours to overnight at the beginning of a firing to insure that the ware is thoroughly dry. This period can start with the burners or electric elements turned very low, or with just a pilot light burning. The door or lid of the kiln can be left partly open during this time. Temperature during the soaking period can reach 100° F to 150° F. During the rise from 150° F to 500° F the temperature should increase only 20° to 25° per hour. From 500° to 1000°, the rise can be from 35° to 40° per hour. At 1000° a glow is visible within the kiln and the cones become perceptible. From 1000° to 1300°, the rise can accelerate to 75° to 100° per hour. From there on, a rise of 100° per hour is quite safe.

For smaller pieces up to 12 inches in height with a wall thickness of ½ inch, the temperature rise may accelerate to 150° F per hour after 1400° F, and later in the cycle 200° F per hour might be feasible. For larger sculptures over 18 inches high with a 1-inch wall thickness, a rise of 100° F per hour should be maintained throughout the firing. Very large sculptures are fired even more slowly. A 10-day firing cycle is common in large commercial kilns.

Flames in close proximity to the ware do not produce adverse effects as long as slow temperature rise is maintained during firing and the damper is properly set for either the strictly oxidizing or reducing atmosphere, as desired. For a clean oxidizing atmosphere, the space between the burner and the air regulator should be a good ½ inch. Each kiln fires differently, so some experimentation will be necessary to learn the proper handling of a new kiln.

For reduction, the burner adjustment can be left as set for oxidation and the damper closed part-way until yellow flames can be seen rising 4 to 6 inches out of the remaining opening. Flames may also come out peephole openings and any cracks in the bricked-up door. During the reduction there may be some carbon monoxide issuing from the kiln, so the room should be well ventilated. The amount of reduction necessary will vary with the effect desired. For a cone 5 firing there can be periods of reduction at cones 1, 3, and 5 which can last 20 minutes to ½ hour. For a cone 10 firing the reduction can last 20 minutes or so and take place at cone 3, 6, and 10. Some artists reduce almost constantly throughout the firing. A 20-minute reduction at the end of the firing may be sufficient. In general, to maintain the maximum reduced effect on the ware, the cooling time should be slightly shorter than the firing time.

For the first firing in a new kiln, place cones in all four bottom corners, on the shelves in the middle of the kiln, and on all four corners on shelves at the very top. It might be well to place brick on all the shelves to serve as ballast rather than risking the work in this first firing. Glaze samples should be liberally included throughout the kiln to see what effects are obtained. This first firing should be a slow one so the kiln will not be placed under undue strain as its mortar joints settle and solidify.

Accuracy of firing is of prime importance. Be sure the cones are visible through the peepholes and that the right ones have been chosen and are correctly placed in the plaque of clay. Watch must be kept on the kiln all through its firing and especially toward the end in order to turn it off at the right time. Overfiring of a kiln can ruin the work of months.

A kiln nearing its final temperature should be checked every few minutes. The kiln should not be opened until it is down to 200° F at the top, or hottest part, to avoid thermal shock to the ware.

COOLING

The cooling of the sculptures within the kiln is important, too. In a muffle kiln— that is, a kiln with an inner wall to separate the burner flames and gases from the ware—the damper is closed upon completion of the firing to hold the heat in and the presence of the muffle further slows the cooling. In open-fire kilns without muffles, further precautions are sometimes necessary. Not only should the damper be pulled shut, but the stack should be closed with a lid to stop the flow of cool air into the kiln. The room in which the kiln is fired should be closed if it is feasible, or brick can be placed around the burner ports to prevent drafts of air being sucked into the cooling kiln. Sculpture that is cooled too rapidly may form hairline cracks, called "dunting," from thermal shock.

LOADING

Loading the sculpture into the kiln for firing requires great care and attention to detail. There should be a space of from ⅜ to ½ inch between sculptures. Remember that a piece that has been bisqued before the glaze firing will not shrink as much as a sculpture that is being fired for the first time, so be sure protruding parts of one sculpture will not shrink down on some other work during the firing. All hollow sculptures must be vented to allow steam to escape easily—beware of explosions. Be sure that sculptures do not wobble on the shelf. If a base is uneven, a shim of old kiln wash or a fragment of kiln wadding may be used to stabilize it.

7
Finishes

The finishes possible for ceramic sculpture are so varied that a whole lifetime of work could not exhaust them all. Several different approaches are presented here in the hope that the beginner will, through experiment, discover many others.

ENGOBES

Engobes, or slips, are a simple and effective means of obtaining color on a piece of sculpture. An engobe is a liquid mixture of clay and coloring material, sometimes with a little flux added, which is painted or sprayed onto the sculpture while it is still leather-hard. The engobe may be an allover color or used only in a few areas for accent. It may be the final finish or, when used under a glaze, it may blend into the glaze for pleasing, subtle effects.

An engobe may be made from the same clay as that used to build the sculpture itself, but without the grog, which might roughen the surface unnecessarily. If the sculpture clay fires to a very light color the engobe may be tinted a variety of colors with the oxides of metals or with the body stains which give the yellows, blues, and greens. If the sculpture clay is a red or brown color the engobe may be darkened further by adding iron oxide, burnt umber, or manganese carbonate. If a light engobe is needed to contrast with a dark sculpture clay some other light-colored clay, such as a buff burning fire clay, may be chosen.

When using an engobe over an entire surface, the difference in amount of shrinkage between the engobe and the clay body must be considered. Both should shrink the same amount during firing. If the engobe shrinks more, it will crack.

If the sculpture shrinks more, the engobe will be loose and will spall off. To reduce shrinkage in an engobe, add 2 to 10 per cent silica to the following formulas. To encourage shrinkage in an engobe, add 1 to 2 per cent bentonite or 5 to 10 per cent ball clay. Actually, the simplest way to use an engobe is for making accents or surface contrast on a textured sculpture. Apply it over the entire surface and, when it is leather hard, scrape it off the ridges and protrusions. It then makes little difference whether it tends to shrink more or less than the sculpture.

A little flux can also be added to the engobe to improve its adherence to the sculpture. From 5 to 10 per cent of a low-fire frit may be added to a cone 04 engobe, or 5 to 15 per cent feldspar to a cone 5 to 10 engobe. (A frit is a combination of ceramic materials melted together and then ground to powder, which can be used to flux clays or glazes.) If a speckle is desired 5 per cent fine iron sand, 40- to 80-mesh iron filings, or ilmenite may be added. An addition of 2 per cent manganese dioxide will give a good fine-grained fleck.

Following is a list of colorants, each one of which, when added to the engobe or clay color coat, will give approximately the hue listed. In some cases, indicated by a bracket, two or more ingredients are needed for the specified color. The colors obtained vary greatly with temperature and with the clay used, so samples should always be fired before the mixture is tried on the actual sculpture. Additions for cone 5 are suggested here. Lower temperatures need more colorant and higher firings need less.

COLORED ENGOBE FORMULAS

Per cent

Tan
Red iron oxide	2.5
Black iron oxide	2
(Slightly grey with fleck)	
Yellow ochre	3
Burnt umber	2
Raw umber	2
Manganese carbonate	1.2

Red
Red iron oxide	7-10

Blue
Cobalt glaze stain	5

Brown
Black iron oxide	12.5
Burnt umber	10.5
Raw umber	10.5
Manganese carbonate	7
[Yellow ochre	10.5]
[Burnt umber	2]

Light gray
Iron chromate	2
[Cobalt oxide	0.2]
[Manganese dioxide	1]

Dark red
Red iron oxide	15

Blue-green
Celadon glaze stain	12

Dark gray
Iron chromate	5
or	
Manganese dioxide	5

Yellow
Yellow glaze stain	8-10
Vanadium stain	5-10

Black

$$\begin{bmatrix} \text{Black glaze stain} & \ldots & \ldots & 4\text{-}5 \\ \text{Manganese dioxide} & \ldots & \ldots & 4\text{-}5 \end{bmatrix}$$

or

$$\begin{bmatrix} \text{Black glaze stain} & \ldots & \ldots & 4 \\ \text{Black iron oxide} & \ldots & \ldots & 4 \end{bmatrix}$$

SLIP CLAYS AS GLAZES

Clays containing natural impurities which are still quite reliable as clay bodies in low fire may melt completely at stoneware temperatures and form beautiful glazes. These are called "slip clays." Michigan and Albany slip are examples of such clays, but countless others may be found in different parts of the country. Such clay-glazes often need no additions to produce fine results. Sometimes they flow too freely at a given temperature and a little kaolin will stiffen them. They may not melt quite enough, in which case whiting, zinc, lead, or a low-fire frit may be added. All slip glazes must be applied to raw, leather-dry clay, since they shrink with the clay body. If applied to dry or bisqued clay, minute cracks appear as the moisture leaves the slip and it shrinks. These minute cracks often do not heal during the firing and leave ugly scars.

CLAY TEXTURES

If a richer, more textured surface is preferred to that obtained by engobes, let us consider colored clay mixtures which may be modeled directly onto the sculptured form. The same clay and grog mix should be used for these color coats as is used to model the sculpture. Otherwise shrinkage difference between the main structure and the color coat may cause surface cracks or even spalling off of the surface coat. The grog content of more highly fluxed color coats may be increased somewhat to cut down their excessive shrinkage.

When applying the color mixture, score the surface of the sculpture well, dampen it with a sponge, and press the colored clay firmly into the prepared area. The coat being applied should be of about the same firmness as the sculpture so that shrinkage will be equal. The color coat should be ⅛ to ¼ inch thick and spread smoothly or applied in little pellets for a rougher effect. Sometimes a little wood block or a fragment of sponge brick can be used to tamp the clay to the desired texture. This method can be an allover treatment of one color, several colors, or of glazed areas next to colored clay areas. Below are some simple color formulas compounded for use at cone 5. They can be modified for use at other temperatures. For a similar effect at cone 04 add 2 to 4 per cent more of the color stains and frit 2106. For use at cones 8 to 10 reduce the colors 2 to 5 per cent and leave out frit 2106. Again, test your color mix on a little slab of sculpture clay before you use it on the final sculpture to be sure you have a good fit between the clays.

Color coat formulas

Per cent

Yellow

Fire clay	65
Grog (20- to fine-mesh)	15
Frit 2106	10*
Yellow stain 308	9**
Yellow ochre	1

Red

Fire clay	58
Grog (20- to fine-mesh)	25
Frit 2106	2*
Red iron oxide	15

Blue

Fire clay	70
Grog (20- to fine-mesh)	15
Celadon stain 103	12**
Frit 2106	3*

Black

Fire clay	55
Grog (20- to fine-mesh)	32
Black stain 801	4**
Manganese dioxide	4
Frit 2106	5*

Tan

Fire clay	65
Grog (20- to fine-mesh)	20
Yellow stain 308	5**
Burnt umber	1
Red iron oxide	1
Frit 2106	8

Chocolate brown

Fire clay	50
Grog (20- to fine-mesh)	28
Burnt umber	6
Red iron oxide	6
Frit 2106	10

*Materials obtained from L. H. Butcher Co., Los Angeles, Calif.
**Materials obtained from B. F. Wagner & Co., Pasadena, Calif.

Interesting textural effects can be obtained by using colored grogs in the clay body or color coat mix. Commercial grogs can be found in white, buff, and red. Other colors may be made by pulverizing and screening scrap brick or tile fragments. Dark brown or black grog can be made by mixing metallic oxides with clay and water, drying the mixture, pulverizing it, and sifting it through a 20-mesh screen. The resulting granules can be placed in a bisqued container and fired to cone 08, after which they can be added to a color mix for application to the surface of a sculpture. The sculpture can be fired to a temperature at which the black grog will melt and form glossy specks on the surface. Any of the oxides and color pigments described may be used to make colored grogs. Plastic Body No. 5 clay makes a good white grog. Albany or Michigan slip clays will give glossy black or yellow-green specks, respectively, when used as grog at cones 8 to 10.

The color and texture imparted by the grog can be made more apparent by sponging the finished leather-dry sculpture lightly to expose more of the particles at the surface. Another technique is to grind the surface of the sculpture with an emery stone after firing to achieve a terrazzo effect.

For a deliberately porous texture,

similar to that of sponge brick, sawdust, ground cork, coffee grounds, or similar material may be added to the clay. This material burns out during the firing, leaving tiny craters in its place. It may be put in the clay body mix, the surface coat, or on certain accent areas.

GLAZES

In considering the glaze to be used for a piece of sculpture, make sure its color, texture, and degree of matness or gloss are suitable to the design and subject matter of the sculpture. Sometimes the very design of the sculpture is intended as a vehicle to display the qualities of a favorite glaze. The glaze can be chosen to give just the right richness to a certain combination of ceramic forms. Glaze can be used in some focal area such as the head, and around the eyes, leaving the clay body exposed elsewhere. Special areas may be incised and filled with glaze, as in cloisonné. The colored engobes or clay textures described earlier may be painted or worked over part of the sculpture and glaze used in other areas, over the engobes and clay textures. The color in the slips and clay textures will come through the glaze, producing beautiful free effects.

Impurities in the clay body, either natural or artificially introduced, will often enter the glaze with beautiful results. A reduction atmosphere can bring the impurities into the glaze more dramatically than an oxidizing atmosphere. In unrefined clays the impurities most often consist of some form of iron oxide with traces of manganese or copper. Controlled impurities can be added to pure commercial fire clays to achieve results similar to those obtained with the materials mentioned in the section on clays and engobes. Any of these added to the base clay will tend to spread into the glaze during firing and lend richness to the final result.

Glazes themselves can be variously colored by the oxides and carbonates of metals and by the myriad glaze stains commercially available. The stains and carbonates produce an even color tone, and the oxides, especially black iron oxide, nickel oxide, and manganese dioxide, are more coarsely ground and produce a definite speckle.

Other granular materials may be added to the glaze to produce more dominant flecks. One is iron sand, which gives a strong black fleck in any glaze and at cones 8 to 10 will often give a beautiful red hue to glazes. Bronze or copper filings will produce black spots with greenish streaks, either when present in the clay body or when added to the glaze, and iron filings in the glaze give black spots with brown streaks. The metal filings added should be fairly fine (between 40- and 80-mesh), unless a very rough, vigorous effect is desired, since larger metal particles tend to melt and bubble out on the surface, causing rounded welts. Granular ilmenite in the glaze will give black spots $\frac{1}{16}$ to $\frac{1}{8}$ inch in diameter. Often 1 per cent is enough to produce interesting effects.

A double application of glaze is another method of achieving richness and depth of color. To the base glaze, mat or glossy, iron or Albany slip up to about 25 per cent may be added. This mixture of base glaze and coloring matter is painted or sprayed on the sculpture to a thickness of about $\frac{1}{16}$ inch on small sculpture and up to $\frac{1}{8}$ inch on very large sculpture. When it dries, an equal coat of base glaze without the iron or Albany slip is then applied.

This glaze can be tinted slightly with 2 per cent vanadium stain to obtain yellow or 1 to 2 per cent copper to obtain green. During the firing the first coat, with its greater amount of flux, will melt through the stiffer outer coat and blend in varied and fascinating ways. Further variation can be achieved by using the base glaze and its additives in some areas and the base alone in others—or by

leaving the clay body itself exposed in still other areas. The glaze application thus becomes an integral part of the design of the sculpture.

Depending on the type of glaze used, ceramic sculpture may be glazed either in the raw, wet stage, when bone-dry, or after it has been bisque-fired to a low temperature. A glaze applied to wet or dry unfired sculpture is called "greenware glaze." Greenware glazes are extremely satisfactory to work with, because the unity between clay and glaze often results in very soft, rich qualities and an economy of effort in the single firing. A greenware glaze should contain about 5 per cent bentonite, substituted for that amount of kaolin or ball clay in the formulas on pages 85-86. This addition will cause it to adhere more tightly to the clay body and shrink uniformly with the sculpture during drying and firing. Slip glazes such as Albany or Michigan slip should be applied to wet ware, but many greenware glazes can be sprayed directly onto the dry, unfired sculpture. This reduces the chance of unequal shrinkage between sculpture and glaze.

Spraying gives the most even coverage for a sculpture that is to be entirely covered with one glaze tone. A pastel fixative sprayer is excellent for spraying sculpture and can be inserted into the compressor hose opening and held with a piece of tape. The rather large opening of the fixitive sprayer permits the spraying of coarse—as well as fine-ground—glazes and glazes with granular materials added. Thus there is no need for a complex glaze gun. The spray can be controlled by adding more or less water, as needed, to keep the mixture at the right consistency. This kind of spraying requires from 30 to 40 pounds of pressure from the compressor. Do not spray too long in one spot or the glaze coat building up will become too wet and, as it dries, may form hairline cracks which sometimes pull apart during the firing. The pulling of the glaze away from the clay is called "crawling" and is a common glaze defect.

Crawling can also be caused by dust on the ware or oil from the hands which is transferred to the sculpture by careless handling. Pieces waiting to be glazed can be protected from dust by a plastic drop cloth and handled with gloves or a cloth. Sometimes a glaze will crawl if the surface of the clay is too smooth. To correct this a texture tool may be used in the final modeling to roughen the surface slightly. If a glaze crawls because it is too stiff, 5 per cent whiting may be added to flux the area next to the clay so that the glaze will adhere to the body.

Glazes which contain little clay or high percentages of water-soluble ingredients such as borax, boric acid, or soda ash cannot be applied to raw, wet clay, because they spall off during drying and crawl or blister during firing. They can be applied safely to bisqued, or fired, surfaces. When the sculpture has been glazed, it must be fired again, but the second firing can proceed at a faster rate.

If a compressor is not available, glazes can be brushed onto the sculpture. The first coat should be applied quite thinly and rubbed well with the finger to fill up all pores. The next coat can be somewhat thicker, but it too should be rubbed smooth.

The following are mat glaze formulas which, with varying modifications, have been widely used by potters and sculptors and give consistently good results.

Raw or bisque ware—Cones 1 to 6

	Grams
Lead carbonate	165.
Feldspar	107.5
Kaolin	72.5
Wollastonite	41.7
Zinc oxide	12.5
Silica	7.5

Tin oxide	7.2
Rutile	3.5
Bentonite	3.2

Use thin layer of undercoat to avoid excessive fluxing of glaze. Do not overfire. Do not reduce.

Suggested Undercoats:
Undercoat #1
75 per cent base glaze
5 per cent copper carbonate
15 per cent red iron oxide
5 per cent Albany slip
or
Undercoat #2
80 per cent base glaze
20 per cent iron oxide

Raw or bisque ware—Cones 5 to 10

	Grams for oxidation	Grams for reduction
Feldspar	52	52
Silica	6	8
Whiting	20	20
Zinc	9	9
Kaolin	10	16
Bentonite	5	5
Zircopax	0	3

Suggested Undercoats:
Undercoat #1
75 per cent base glaze
25 per cent red iron oxide
or
Undercoat #2
65 per cent base glaze
10 per cent red iron oxide
15 per cent Albany slip
5 per cent Manganese dioxide
5 per cent copper carbonate

Ash glaze—for raw or bisque ware— Cones 7 to 9

	Grams
Feldspar	50
Ash	50
Ball clay	12.5
Bentonite	12.5
Zinx oxide	3 to 7

Any kind of wood ash may be used in these glazes. Mix ash with water. Let settle and pour off water. Repeat three times. Put ash through a 20-, a 40- and a 60-mesh screen. Weigh out when dry.

Ash glaze—raw or bisque ware—Cone 04

	Grams
Lead carbonate	70
Feldspar	45
Ball clay	45
Kaolin	1.5
Bentonite	4.5
Wood ash	20

Raw or bisque ware—Cones 6 to 10

	Grams
Feldspar	40
Whiting	22.5
Cornwall stone	20
Kaolin	5
Bentonite	5
Zinc	10.2

Suggested Undercoats:
Undercoat #1
75 per cent base glaze
10 per cent Albany slip
10 per cent black iron oxide
2½ per cent copper carbonate
or
Undercoat #2
75 per cent base glaze
25 per cent red iron oxide

Colors for these glazes can be obtained by adding coloring ingredients as follows:

Light green	2 per cent copper carbonate
Dark green	4 per cent copper carbonate
Grey-green	2 per cent copper carbonate, 2 per cent nickel oxide
Blue	½ per cent cobalt carbonate
Yellow	5 per cent yellow stain or vanadium
Brown	5 per cent red or black iron oxide

Tan	5 per cent rutile or 2 per cent red or black iron oxide
Blue-green	½ per cent cobalt, 2 per cent copper carbonate
Black	5 per cent to 8 per cent black glaze stain
Warmer colors	3 per cent to 4 per cent rutile
Grayer colors	3 per cent to 4 per cent nickel oxide

Sculpture is often most pleasing with a mat surface, but there are times when brilliant, shiny glazes are indispensable. The beaks and feathers of birds, fish, tree and flower forms, and color areas on abstract sculpture often need brilliant accents. A very simple base glaze is as follows:

Raw or bisque ware—Cones 3 to 5

	Grams
Plastic vitrox	48
Colemanite	50
Bentonite	1
Kaolin	2

For color

White (opaque)	2 per cent Kaolin
Green	6 per cent copper carbonate
Blue	6 per cent to 10 per cent blue glaze stain
Yellow	10 per cent yellow glaze stain or vanadium
Tan	2 per cent brown glaze stain
Brown	4 per cent brown glaze stain

This glaze may be brushed on dry, unfired sculpture or on bisqued ware. Rub pinholes with finger after each coat. Three coats give good coverage.

For brilliant reds, oranges, and yellows, a very excellent series of glazes may be obtained from Drakenfeld & Co. (see Appendix II), as follows:

Red-orange	No. 66212
Yellow	No. 66223
Orange	3 parts No. 66212 to 1 part No. 66223

This glaze fires to cone 05. The glaze should be sprayed on bisqued ware. It gives uneven coverage when brushed.

PATINA

Patina is a term which was originally used to describe the finishes on bronze, acquired either by natural weathering or by acid treatment. It has since come to have a wider application and now refers to finishes, other than glaze or fired clay texture, which are applied to the surface of a sculpture after firing.

To apply a patina, the sculpture is first stained the desired color. The coloring agents are varied. Oxides and carbonates of metals may be mixed with paste floor wax and rubbed into the surface of the sculpture. Or oil paint thinned with turpentine for deep penetration may be painted on the sculpture and given a coat of wax when dry. If the sculpture is already a good color but needs a sheen, a light coat of clear wax may be applied. When the wax and color coats are dry—one to two days is sufficient—a coat of slip is applied. This can be made from any fire clay or ball clay and water. Slip should be the consistency of very thick cream. It is applied to the sculpture with a stiff brush and worked into all crevices and textures so that no clay body color shows through. It can also be rubbed into the sculpture surface with the fingers. One coat is enough and should be just thick enough to cover the surface completely. If it is too thick it may scale off as it dries.

When the slip coat is dry it is ready for polishing. Stiff cleaning brushes are suitable for the purpose and toothbrushes are excellent for rubbing areas that larger brushes cannot reach. The slip-covered sculpture is rubbed briskly with the brushes until the excess slip is removed. The mild abrasive action of the clay slip imparts a dull luster to the revealed clay surface, and the slip remaining on textured areas gives handsome contrast. The ceramic is finished when fired.

Slip may also be used to "antique" a rough textured ceramic. Apply slip, as above, but wipe it from protruding areas with a damp sponge. When it is dry, burnish the protrusions and fire the ceramic.

WATERPROOFING

Ceramic sculpture which is to be placed out of doors in climates where temperature drops below 32° F should be protected against the elements by a waterproofing treatment which will completely seal the pores of the clay. This vastly increases the durability of the sculpture without affecting its appearance. Thawing and freezing are an immediate threat to glazed or unglazed ceramic sculpture, but a thorough waterproofing job can check entirely the ravages of frost.

The waterproofing solution must be composed of some kind of inert compound dissolved in a thin, nonaqueous solvent. The solvent carries the compound deeply into the pores of the clay and deposits it there as evaporation takes place. The compound must be insoluble in water and must remain in the pores, sealing them against any infiltration of water.

There are numerous waterproofing compounds on the market which will successfully prepare ceramic sculptures. The compound chosen should be a colorless, transparent one so that the body color of the clay is not changed. In most cases, since the solvent evaporates after the first application, the compound shrinks, necessitating a second and sometimes a third coat to insure complete saturation. Some compounds undergo a slight chemical change upon the evaporation of the solvent and will expand slightly, filling the air spaces tightly. In this case one coat is sufficient.

The presence of heat either in the sculpture or the waterproofing mixture will materially aid the penetration of the solution. If the sculpture is too large to be heated in an oven or kiln, a blow torch may be gently applied to heat the areas to which the solution is being applied. Care should be taken not to overheat any area, because the clay can crack under too great or too sudden an application of heat. A simpler heating method is to place the sculpture in the sun on a hot day. The minimum temperature at which waterproofing application is advisable is always printed on the can. In general it should not be applied at less than 70° F.

Fatty oils and petroleum distillates make very good waterproofing materials. Paraffin is an excellent example. It is very inert and does not deteriorate with time. Paraffin mixtures should be applied hot to a heated surface for deepest penetration, since paraffin solidifies readily upon cooling. Paraffin in combination with creosote, in a solvent of turpentine, has successfully preserved the Egyptian Obelisk, Cleopatra's Needle, against the severe climate of New York City for over 95 years.

GALLERY OF EXAMPLES BY THE AUTHOR

Monkey Grille, height 72 inches.
Red quarry tile clay; black-and-white slip
applied with brush. Oxidized at cone 5.
Installed in National Insurance
Association Building, Los Angeles.
Photo by Burton Frasher.

Deer Drinking, height 40 inches. Glazed terra cotta. Fired in oxidation to cone 9.

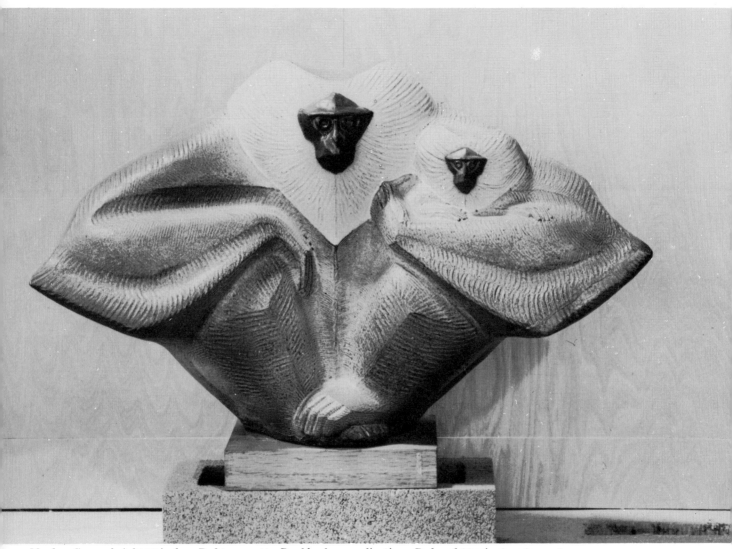

Monkey Group, height 21 inches. Red terra cotta. Double glaze application. Reduced 20 minutes at cone 5.

Gibbons, height 32 inches (entire panel 8 feet high).
Red terra cotta, glazed. Fired in oxidation to cone 5.

Civet Cats, height 28 inches. Clay mixture: 75% Lincoln Fire Clay,
25% grog. Color coat contains black and white grog.

Crouching Bear, height 26 inches. Clay mixture: 75% Lincoln Fire Clay, 25% grog. Color bearing coat added in brown and tan with black grog.

Tiger, length 10 feet. Terra cotta with colored clay applied to surface. Poured solid with concrete and steel.

Toucans, height 16 inches. Clay mixture: 75% Lincoln
Fire Clay, 25% grog. Color coat modeled on surface.

Deer Group, height 38 inches.
Glazed terra cotta.

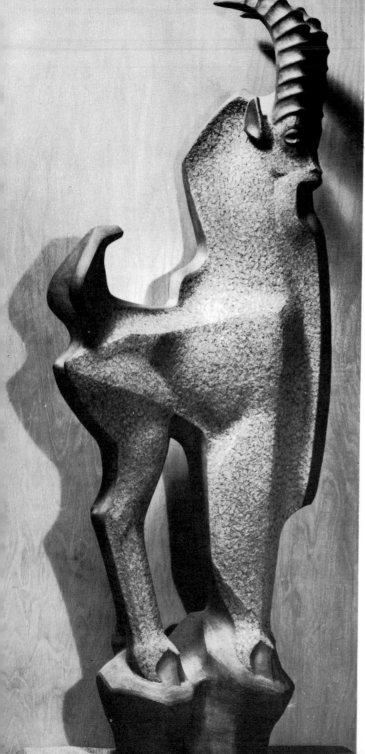

Jonah and the Whale, height 27 inches.
Terra cotta with tan and yellow glaze.

Ibex, height 43 inches. Terra cotta with
applied golden clay texture.

APPENDIX I.

*Temperature Equivalents of Cones
to Cone 20*

Cone	Centigrade	Fahrenheit
022	585	1085
021	595	1103
020	625	1157
019	630	1166
018	670	1238
017	720	1328
016	735	1355
015	770	1418
014	795	1463
013	825	1517
012	840	1544
011	875	1607
010	890	1634
09	930	1706
08	945	1733
07	975	1787
06	1005	1841
05	1030	1886
04	1050	1922
03	1080	1976
02	1095	2003
01	1110	2030
1	1125	2057
2	1135	2075
3	1145	2093
4	1165	2129
5	1180	2156
6	1190	2174
7	1210	2210
8	1225	2237
9	1250	2282
10	1260	2300
11	1285	2345
12	1310	2390
13	1350	2462
14	1390	2534
15	1410	2570
16	1450	2642
17	1465	2669
18	1485	2705
19	1515	2759
20	1520	2768

APPENDIX II.

Sources of Supply

BUILDERS AND SUPPLIERS OF KILNS, KILN
FURNITURE, AND REFRACTORY MATERIALS

Carborundum Company, Perth Amboy,
N. J. Kiln furniture and shelves.
Denver Fire Clay Co., Denver, Colo.
(Branches in El Paso, Tex.,
Salt Lake City, Utah) Kilns.
Electro Refractories and Alloys Corp.,
344 Delaware Ave., Buffalo 2, N. Y.
Shelves and kiln furniture.
General Refractories, Vernon, Calif.
Fire clay, fire brick, grog.
Harper Electric Furnace Corp., Buffalo,
N. Y. Electric kilns.
The Louthan Manufacturing Co., East
Liverpool, Ohio. Kiln furniture.
Mendell Kilns, 12330 East Rush Street,
El Monte, Calif. Kilns of all types.
New Castle Refractories, New Castle, Pa.
Kiln furniture.
Nordstrom Kilns, 9046 Garvey, South
San Gabriel, Calif.
Norton Co., Worcester 6, Mass. Heavy-
duty refractories.
Ohio Kilns, Granville, Ohio. Kilns of
all types.
Pereco Electric Kiln, 893 Chambers Road,
Columbus 12, Ohio. Electric kilns.
West Coast Kiln Co., 635 Vineland Ave.,
La Puente, Calif.

PRODUCERS OF CLAY

American Art Clay Co., Indianapolis, Ind.
J. M. Huber Corp., 630 Third Ave., New
York 17, N. Y.
United Clay Mines Corp., Trenton, N. J.

SUPPLIERS OF CERAMIC CLAYS, GLAZES,
KILNS, TOOLS, CONES

L. H. Butcher Co., 3628 East Olympic
Blvd., Los Angeles, Calif. Ceramic
supplies of all kinds.
Columbian Carbon Co., 380 Madison Ave.,
New York 17, N. Y. Oxides and coloring
materials.

Drakenfeld & Co., New York, N. Y.
Glazes, glaze stains, coloring pigments.
Edward Orton Ceramic Foundation,
1445 Summit Street, Columbus 1, Ohio.
Pyrometric cones.
Ferro Corp., Cleveland, Ohio. Enamel
colors, glazes, frits.
Glostex Chemicals, Inc., 3056 Bandini
Blvd., Los Angeles 23, Calif. Frits.
Hanop Chemical Service Co., Columbus
15, Ohio. General ceramic materials.
Hanovia Chemical and Manufacturing
Co., Newark, N. J. Ceramic materials.
Harshaw Chemical Co., 1945 East 97th
Street, Cleveland, Ohio. Ceramic materials.
Italian Terra Cotta Co., 1149 Mission
Road, Los Angeles 33, Calif. Several kinds
of sculpture clay.
M. Martini, Milton, N. Y. Italian sculpture
modeling, and ceramic steel tools.
O'Hommel Co., Pittsburgh 3, Pa. General
ceramic materials.
Pemco Corp., Baltimore, Md. Frits, glazes,
enamels, stains.
Sculpture Associates, 101 St. Marks Place,
New York 9, N. Y. Sculpture tools of
all kinds.
Sculpture House, 38 East 30th Street,
New York 16, N. Y. Tools and sculpture
supplies.
Thomas C. Thompson, Highland Park, Ill.
Enamels, frits, glazes.
Vitro Manufacturing Co., Pittsburgh 4,
Pa. Ceramic color specialists.
B. F. Wagner Co., 186 North Vernon
Ave., Pasadena 3, Calif. General ceramic
materials.
S. Paul Ward, Inc., 601-605 Mission
Street, South Pasadena, Calif. General
ceramic materials.
Westwood Ceramic Supply Co., 610 Venice
Blvd., Venice, Calif. General ceramic
materials, clay.
Zircoa-Zirconium Corp. of America, P. O.
Box 9583, Cleveland 39, Ohio. Opacifiers
of many kinds.

PUBLICATIONS GIVING ADDITIONAL SOURCES
OF CERAMIC MATERIALS

Brick and Clay Record. Industrial
Publications, Inc., 5 South Wabash Ave.,
Chicago 3, Ill.
Ceramic Data Book. Industrial
Publications, Inc., 5 South Wabash Ave.,
Chicago 3, Ill.
Ceramic Industry. Industrial Publications,
Inc., 5 South Wabash Ave., Chicago 3, Ill.
Ceramic News. Iander Publications,
239 South Robertson Blvd., Beverly Hills,
Calif.

APPENDIX III.

Bibliography

SOURCE BOOKS

Human and animal anatomy:

Bridgman, G. B. *Constructive Anatomy.*
Pelham, N. Y.: Bridgman Publishers,
Inc., 11th printing, 1941.
Ellenberger and Braun. *Anatomy of
Animals.* Meridan, Conn.: The Meridan
Gravure Co., 2nd printing, 1947.
Knight, C. R. *Animal Anatomy and
Psychology for the Artist and Layman.*
New York and London: McGraw-Hill
Book Co., Inc., 1947.
Putnam, Brenda. *The Sculptor's Way.*
New York and Toronto: Farrar and
Rinehart, 1939.

Sculpture:

Goldscheider, Ludwig. *Michelangelo.* New
York: Phaidon Publishers, Inc., 4th
edition, 1962.
Mestrovic, Ivan. *The Sculpture of Ivan
Mestrovic.* Syracuse, N. Y.: Syracuse
University Press, 1948.
Zorach, William. *Zorach Explains
Sculpture.* New York: American Artists
Group, latest printing, 1960.

Techniques of handling clay and glazes:

Binns, C. F. *The Potter's Craft.* New
York: D. Van Nostrand Co., 3rd edition,
1947.
Leach, Bernard. *A Potter's Book.* London:
Faber & Faber, Ltd., 1946.
Rhodes, Daniel. *Clay and Glazes for the
Potter.* New York and Philadelphia:
Chilton Co., Book Division. 3rd printing,
1959.

Nature references:

Andrews, Roy Chapman. *All About
Strange Beasts of the Past.* Random
House, 1956.
Andrews, Roy Chapman. *All About
Whales.* Random House, 1954.
Andrews, Roy Chapman. *All About
Dinosaurs.* Random House, 1953.
Blossfeldt, Karl von. *Urformen der Kunst.*
Berlin and Tübingen: Ernst Verlag,
Wasmuth, 1948.
Bourlière, François. *Mammals of the
World: Their Life and Habits.* New York:
Alfred A. Knopf, 1955.
Bridges, William. *Golden Book of Zoo
Animals.* Golden Press.
Buchsbaum, Ralph. *Living Invertebrates
of the World.* Garden City, N. Y.:
Doubleday & Co., Inc., 1960.
Buchsbaum, Ralph and Milne, Lorus J.
The Lower Animals. Garden City, N. Y.:
Doubleday & Co., Inc., 1960.
Cochran, D. M. *Living Amphibians of the
World.* Garden City, N. Y.: Doubleday &
Co., Inc., 1961.
Cornell, Henrik. *Carl Milles and the
Milles Gardens.* Boston Book.
Ellenberger, Wilhelm & others. *Atlas of
Animal Anatomy for Artists.* Dover, 1957.
The Epic of Man. Patricia Hunt, ed. New
York: Time, Inc., 1960.
Gilliard, T. E. *Living Birds of the World.*
Garden City, N. Y.: Doubleday & Co., Inc.,
1958.
*The Golden Book Encyclopedia of Natural
Science.* Herbert S. Zim, ed. 16 volumes.
New York: The Golden Press, Inc., 1962.
Gould, John. *Tropical Birds.* London,
Toronto and Sydney: B. T. Batsford, Ltd.,
1955.
Hegner, Robert. *Parade of the Animal
Kingdom.* New York: The Macmillan Co.,
1935.
Herald, E. S. *Living Fishes of the World.*
Garden City, N. Y.: Doubleday & Co., Inc.,
1961.
Huxley, Julian. *Kingdom of the Beasts.*
New York: The Vanguard Press, 1956.
Klots, A. B. *Living Insects of the World.*
Garden City, N. Y.: 1959.

Klots, Alexander B. *Field Guide to the
Butterflies.* Houghton, 1951.
Klots, Alexander B. *World of Butterflies*

& Moths. Houghton, 1958.

Knight, Charles R. Animal Drawing: Anatomy and Action for Artists. Dover, 1959.

Life Nature Library Series. Patricia Hunt, ed. New York: Time, Inc., 1962.

Life's Picture History of Western Man. Patricia Hunt, ed. New York: Time, Inc., 1960.

Murphy, R. C., and Dean Amadon. Land Birds of America. New York and London: McGraw-Hill Book Co., Inc., 1953.

Pinney, Roy. Golden Book of Wild Animal Pets. Golden Press.

Raphael, Max. Pre-Historic Cave Paintings. New York: Pantheon Books-Marchbanks Press, 1945.

Sanderson, I. T. Living Mammals of the World. Garden City, N. Y.: Doubleday & Co., Inc., 1955.

Sanderson, Ivan T. How to Know the American Mammals. New American Library, 1951.

Schmidt, K. P. Living Reptiles of the World. Garden City, N. Y.: Doubleday & Co., Inc., 1957.

Smith, J. L. B. The Sea Fishes of Southern Africa. Central News Agency, Ltd., South Africa, 1953.

Suschitzky, W. The Golden Book of Animals. New York: The Golden Press, 1958.

The World We Live In. Patricia Hunt, ed. New York: Time, Inc., 1960.

The World's Great Religions. Patricia Hunt, ed. New York: Time, Inc., 1960.

The Wonders of Life on Earth. Patricia Hunt, ed. New York: Time, Inc., 1960.

Ylla. Animals. New York: Hastings House.

Ylla. Animals in Africa. New York: Harper & Brothers.

Ylla and Arthur Gregor. Animal Babies. Harper, 1959.

Ylla and Crosby Newell. Polar Bear Brothers. Harper, 1960.

Glossary

ball clay—fine grained clay used to give plasticity to a clay body

bisqued ware—a ceramic that has been fired once

body stain—color in a clay body obtained by mixing metallic oxides or salts in it

crawling—a glaze defect characterized by globules of glaze, leaving exposed the clay body

dunting—small hairline cracks that form when a clay has cooled too rapidly after firing

earthenware—a low firing, generally reddish clay that is relatively soft and porous when fired. Fired below cone 1

engobe—slip, or liquid clay, used as a surface colorant

flowing glaze—a glaze that is very fluid at its maturing temperature

flux—a ceramic material used to lower the melting point of a clay or glaze

frit—a glassy compound that has been partly or wholly fused by heat. It is ground and used in glazes to overcome spalling due to improper fit.

glaze—a combination of ceramic materials which, when fired to a maturing temperature, becomes a glassy substance. The fired glaze may be mat, or non-shiny, or glossy.

greenware—a bone dry ceramic that has not been fired

greenware glaze—a glaze compounded to fit unfired clay

grog—finely ground fire brick that has been screened (meshed)

kiln wadding—an unfired mixture of refractory clays used for propping kiln furniture

kiln wash—a watery mixture of flint and china clay that is painted on the top surface of shelves to protect them against glaze drippings

mat glaze—a glaze that when fired has a non-shiny finish

muffle—the part of a kiln that separates the wares from the flames

oxidation firing—a technique in which the products of combustion are not allowed to reach the ware being fired

patina—a surface treatment on unfired or fired clays that makes them shinier and darker

plaque—a pad of kiln wadding used to hold pyrometric cones

reduction firing—a technique in which the products of combustion are allowed to enter the chamber and combine with the ceramic ware

slip—highly liquid clay used to adhere two surfaces or as an engobe

slip clays—low fire clays which, when fired at high temperatures, form a glaze. Used as engobes

stiff glaze—a glaze that may need flux, if not purposely made non-flowing

stoneware—high firing clay that is very strong, hard, and glassy when fired

Index